Philip Kerr, Sue Kay & '

American
Inside Out

Workbook

Pre-intermediate

MACMILLAN

Macmillan Education
Between Towns Road, Oxford OX4 3PP, UK
A division of Macmillan Publishers Limited
Companies and representatives throughout the world

ISBN 1 405 02455 0

First published 2002
American Edition 2004

Project management by Desmond O'Sullivan, ELT Publishing Services
Edited by Alyson Maskell, Phoenix Publishing Services
Designed by Jackie Hill at 320 Design
Illustrated by Martin Chatterton pp. 12, 22, 51, 62, 65, 81; Mark Thomas
pp. 15, 75; Ed McLachlan pp. 17, 29, 47, 64, 69, 77; Julian Mosedale
pp. 21, 37, 79; Shelagh McNicholas pp. 26, 43, 46, 83.
Cover design by Andrew Oliver
Cover painting *After Visiting David Hockney* © Howard Hodgkin

The authors and publishers would like to thank the following for
permission to reproduce copyright material:

Excerpts on pp. 19, 68 from *The Mammoth Book of Jokes* edited by Geoff
Tibballs (Robinson, 2000), reprinted by permission of Constable &
Robinson Publishing Ltd; excerpt on p. 72 (bottom right) from *Collins
Gem Book: Ghosts* by Karen Hurrell and Janet Bord (HarperCollins, 2000),
reprinted by permission of HarperCollins Publishers Ltd.; excerpt on
p. 73 from *The Unexplained Strange People* by Jamie Stokes (Constable and
Robinson), reprinted by permission of the publisher.

The authors and publishers would like to thank the following for
permission to reproduce their photographs:

Corbis p. 76(t), Corbis/Christopher Cox p. 33, Corbis/James Davis
p. 9(b), Corbis/David Lees p. 55, Corbis/Karen Huntt-Mason p. 9(m),
Corbis/Mona Lisa (1503–1505) Leonardo da Vinci: Gianni Dagli Orti
p. 45, Corbis/Matthew Polak p. 25, Corbis/Vine Streano p. 7(m),
Corbis/Patrick Ward p. 9(t), Corbis–Sygma/Sunset Boulevard p. 48;
FPG p. 71 (goldfish); Hulton Archive pp. 13, 73; Image Bank p. 71 (dog,
hamster); Moviestore p.53; Stone pp. 11, 71(t, cat), 76(b); Telegraph
Colour Library p. 7(t).

Although we have tried to trace and contact copyright holders before
publication, in some cases this has not been possible. If contacted we will
be pleased to rectify any errors or omissions at the earliest opportunity.

Printed and bound in Thailand

2008 2007 2006 2005 2004
10 9 8 7 6 5 4 3 2 1

1 *Me*

Grammar

1 Complete each question with an appropriate question word. Then circle the correct answer.

Example
<u>Who </u> was married to the actor Bruce Willis?

a) Cher   b) Cristina Aguilera (c) Demi Moore)

1 _____ is the actor Nicholas Cage's real last name?
   a) Coppola   b) Lucas   c) Spielberg

2 _____ Beatle was really named Richard Starkey?
   a) John Lennon   b) Paul McCartney
   c) Ringo Starr

3 _____ does Elton John come from?
   a) Edinburgh   b) London   c) New York

4 _____ was the movie *Titanic* made?
   a) 1997   b) 1998   c) 1999

2 The conversation below is with a Web robot (similar to A.L.I.C.E.) named John Lennon. Circle the correct verb form.

A: (Do you miss)/*Miss you* Yoko?
B: Yoko's always in my thoughts.
A: (a) *Argued you/Did you argue* with Paul?
B: No, I didn't argue with Paul. (b) *Is that/That is* important?
A: (c) *Do like you/Do you like* the music of Oasis?
B: I don't know if I like the music of Oasis.
   I love TV shows about the Rolling Stones.
A: What (d) *is your favorite Beatles song?/your favorite Beatles song is?*
B: *Here, There and Everywhere* …just beautiful.
A: (e) *Do you think/Think you* the world is becoming more peaceful?
B: I don't think about it.

3 Insert an auxiliary verb (*do, does, did*) in the questions below **where necessary**. Some of the questions do not need an auxiliary.

Example
Where you learn English?
(did inserted) Where ̭you learn English?

a) How much you weigh?

b) Who speaks the best English in your class?

c) How often your teacher give you homework?

d) What you have for breakfast today?

e) Which languages can you speak?

f) Which party won the last election?

4 Rearrange the words to make questions.

Example
name original Elton John's was What ?
What was Elton John's original name?

a) change David Bowie's did his name son Why ?
   _____
   _____

b) London his after Who section named of daughter a ?
   _____
   _____

c) A.L.I.C.E. does How languages many speak ?
   _____
   _____

d) did John Lennon record *Stand By Me* When ?
   _____
   _____

Now answer the questions. The answers are all in Unit 1 of your Student's Book.

Example
<u>Reginald Kenneth Dwight </u>

a) _____
b) _____
c) _____
d) _____

Reading

1 Read the stories below and match each story to a title.

- **How stupid can you be?**
- **The world's most inappropriate name**
- **Will you marry me?**

a

One day, a man lost his dog. (1) He put an advertisement in the newspaper and hoped that somebody would telephone him with news of his pet. It was easy to identify the dog. It had only three legs and had also lost an ear in a fight with a rottweiler. Unfortunately, the dog was blind, too—the result of a fight with a cat. (2) And if someone found the dog, they could check its name. It had a tag around its neck with its name on it: Lucky!

b

The British conductor Sir Thomas Beecham was walking one day with a friend of his sister's. (3) Her name was Utica Wells. Beecham turned to the young woman and said, "I don't like your first name. I'd like to change it." "You can't do that," she replied, "but you can change my last name." (4) They got married soon afterwards.

c

A woman, Mrs. Smith, was in the hospital after the birth of her son. (5) She was trying to decide what to name her son when she walked past a door. It had the name "KING" on it. That's a good name, she thought. A little later, she walked past another door, and this time she saw the name "NOSMO." (6) But she liked it, too, and so her son was named Nosmo King Smith. It was only six months later that she discovered her terrible mistake.

2 Where do these missing sentences belong in the stories opposite? Write the number in the box.

a) He looked at her and smiled. ☐

b) He was afraid that something terrible had happened. [1]

c) It had no hair on its rear end—after an accident with an electric heater. ☐

d) It was their first date. ☐

e) Strange, but interesting, she thought. ☐

f) When she was feeling well again, she went for a walk. ☐

3 Read the stories again and write questions for the following answers.

Example
Where <u>did the man put an advertisement</u>?

In the newspaper. (*story a*)

a) How many _____
_____?
Three. (*story a*)

b) What _____
_____?
A name tag. (*story a*)

c) What _____
_____?
He was a conductor. (*story b*)

d) Which _____
_____?
Her first name. (*story b*)

e) When _____
_____?
Soon afterwards. (*story b*)

f) Where _____
_____?
On a door. (*story c*)

g) When _____
_____?
Six months later. (*story c*)

Vocabulary

1 Read the information and complete the names on John Lennon's family tree.

- Julian's stepmother is named Yoko.
- Julian's half brother has a partner named Yuka.
- One of John Lennon's half sisters had the same name as his mother.
- Mimi has a niece named Jacqui.
- Sean had a great-grandmother named Mary.

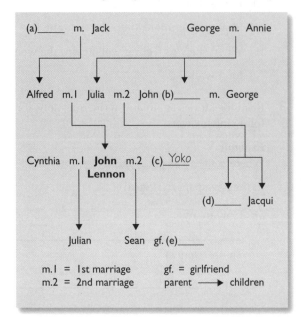

2 Look at the completed family tree and say if the following sentences are true (T) or false (F).

a) John Lennon was Mimi's nephew. ☐

b) Alfred's ex-wife was named Julia. ☐

c) Yoko was Jack's daughter-in-law. ☐

d) Annie was Cynthia's aunt. ☐

e) Julian was Jacqui's stepson. ☐

f) Annie didn't have any great-grandchildren. ☐

g) George's father-in-law was also named George. ☐

h) John Lennon had an uncle named Jack. ☐

3 In the following sentences, delete *like* when it should not be there. Four sentences are correct.

Example
He always looks ~~like~~ terrible early in the morning.

a) He sounds like a very friendly person.

b) My ex-husband looked like a macho cowboy.

c) They looked like a little tired after the lesson.

d) She looks like a typical middle-aged mom.

e) She sounds like foreign—is she Greek?

f) My father-in-law looks like Dracula. Just kidding!

g) You look like stressed out. What's up?

4 Match the sentence beginnings in box A with their endings in box B.

A

a) I think he has nothing
b) In the 1950s, many parents named
c) In the next few days, I need to make
d) Madonna recorded
e) Many people believe
f) She didn't pay
g) The exercise is very easy if you follow
h) They want their children to grow

B

1 a decision about my future.
2 attention, so she didn't understand.
3 her first song in 1982.
4 in common with his girlfriend.
5 up in a safe, quiet place.
6 the simple instructions.
7 their children Susan or Michael.
8 in life after death.

5 Complete each sentence with a word from the box.

nanny   banker   doctor
police officer   psychologist   student
used-car salesman   waiter

a) A _____ buys and sells old cars.

b) A _____ helps people who are sick.

c) A _____ investigates crimes.

d) A _____ has an important position in a bank.

e) A _____ serves food in a restaurant.

f) A _____ studies the human mind.

g) A _____ goes to primary school, secondary school, or college.

h) A _____ takes care of other people's children and does housework.

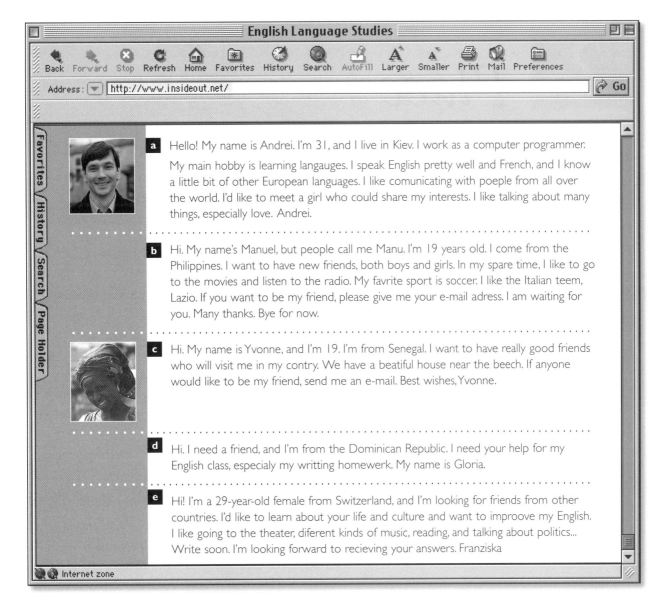

English Language Studies

Address: http://www.insideout.net/

a Hello! My name is Andrei. I'm 31, and I live in Kiev. I work as a computer programmer. My main hobby is learning langauges. I speak English pretty well and French, and I know a little bit of other European languages. I like comunicating with poeple from all over the world. I'd like to meet a girl who could share my interests. I like talking about many things, especially love. Andrei.

b Hi. My name's Manuel, but people call me Manu. I'm 19 years old. I come from the Philippines. I want to have new friends, both boys and girls. In my spare time, I like to go to the movies and listen to the radio. My favrite sport is soccer. I like the Italian teem, Lazio. If you want to be my friend, please give me your e-mail adress. I am waiting for you. Many thanks. Bye for now.

c Hi. My name is Yvonne, and I'm 19. I'm from Senegal. I want to have really good friends who will visit me in my contry. We have a beatiful house near the beech. If anyone would like to be my friend, send me an e-mail. Best wishes, Yvonne.

d Hi. I need a friend, and I'm from the Dominican Republic. I need your help for my English class, especialy my writting homewerk. My name is Gloria.

e Hi! I'm a 29-year-old female from Switzerland, and I'm looking for friends from other countries. I'd like to learn about your life and culture and want to improove my English. I like going to the theater, diferent kinds of music, reading, and talking about politics... Write soon. I'm looking forward to recieving your answers. Franziska

Internet zone

Writing

1 The messages above were posted on a Web site for English language students. Each message has three spelling mistakes. Find the mistakes and correct them.

2 Choose one message and write a short reply (50–80 words).

Pronunciation

1 Match the words in each column that have the same vowel sounds.

are	call	daughter
mean	improve	feel
movie	father	girl
thoughts	learn	grew
world	niece	partner

Listen to the recording to check your answers.

2 What are the words below?

Example

/mi/   me

a) /pɑrt/ _____
b) /wil/ _____
c) /tul/ _____
d) /fɜrst/ _____
e) /bɔrn/ _____

Listen to the recording to check your answers.

2 Place

Grammar

1 Write the plural of each noun in the correct column.

> ~~beach~~   brush   ~~child~~   church   ~~city~~
> ~~vacation~~   man   quality   statue
> summary   taxi   tooth   tourist
> university   watch   woman

Plurals ending in "s"
vacations
_____
_____
_____

Plurals ending in "ies"
cities
_____
_____
_____

Plurals ending in "es"
beaches
_____
_____
_____

Irregular plurals
children
_____
_____
_____

2 Each sentence contains *one* mistake. Correct the mistake.

Example
I'd like some advices about restaurants in the city, please.

a) You need to make more progresses in mathematics!

b) Two customs officers wanted to look at my luggages.

c) The students in the class had a lot of homeworks.

d) There was a lot of informations on TV about the elections in the United States and Mexico.

e) I don't have enough moneys to go to restaurants every day.

f) They bought some breads to make sandwiches.

g) Many Americans enjoy the fresh airs and spectacular views of the Rocky Mountains.

3 Complete each question with *much* or *many*.

Example
How <u>many</u> books did you read last year?

a) How _____ bread do you eat every day?

b) How _____ homework does your teacher give you?

c) How _____ money do you have with you now?

d) How _____ people in your town are unemployed?

e) How _____ progress do you think you will make with your English this year?

f) How _____ restaurants have you been to in your town?

g) How _____ students are there in your school?

Now answer each question. Use a word or phrase from the box.

> a few   a little   a lot   lots   none
> not many   not much   one

4 Complete each sentence about New York with *much, many, a little,* or *a few*.

a) How _____ do you know about New York?

b) New York gets only _____ snow in the winter.

c) Not _____ people in New York speak languages other than English.

d) Only _____ police officers have guns.

e) The mayor makes speeches only _____ times each year.

f) There are too _____ museums to visit in one day.

g) There is not _____ modern architecture.

h) You do not see _____ traffic downtown.

Now decide if sentences b) – h) are true (T) or false (F).

Listening

1 Cover the tapescript opposite and listen to the recording. Which place is the speaker describing?

2 Listen again and decide if the following sentences are true (T) or false (F).

a) He first went to Marrakech four or five years ago. ☐

b) He went there for his summer vacation. ☐

c) He traveled with his girlfriend. ☐

d) He stayed with the family of a friend. ☐

e) After dinner, he visited the Koutoubia Mosque. ☐

f) Djemaa el Fna is the name of his favorite cafe. ☐

g) There is a lot to see in the main square. ☐

h) You can see the Atlas Mountains from the city. ☐

i) He has been there six times. ☐

j) His last visit was three months ago. ☐

Correct the sentences that are false.

I guess the most interesting, and the most exciting, place I've ever been is Marrakech. I first went there many years ago, maybe ten, twelve years, I can't remember exactly. I was living and working in Casablanca, which is, oh, I don't know, about four or five hours from Marrakech. We had a long weekend, and Dave and I—he was my best friend then, we both had the same name, and people called us the two Daves—we were looking for something to do. There was a guy we worked with, Malik, and he invited us to come and stay with his family.

So we all set off on a Thursday evening after work, and eventually we got to Marrakech. His family lives in an amazing house very near the main square, the Djemaa el Fna. His mom cooked us dinner, and then we all went to the market square. We sat on the roof terrace of a cafe, drinking mint tea and watching the action in the square below. It really is the most incredible place in the world. There are people buying and selling absolutely everything. There are lots of little "kitchens" serving soup and kebabs and snails and everything. You can listen to storytellers (if you speak Arabic, that is), watch snake charmers, acrobats, jugglers. On Saturday, I even saw a group of men on camels! Their faces were painted blue, and they had come from the desert in the south of the country.

There are lots of other things to see and do. The Koutoubia Mosque is spectacular, and all the tourists go there. The views are out of this world, with the Atlas Mountains in the distance, and there are some beautiful parks, like the garden that belonged to Yves St. Laurent. It has great restaurants. Everything about it is great.

But it's the square, the Djemaa el Fna, and the shopping streets around it, that make Marrakech really special. Every time I go back to Marrakech, and I've probably been there ten or twelve times, I go straight to the square and sit on my favorite cafe terrace. If I ever have the money, I'd love to buy a house there. But for now, it's just a dream. Right now, I don't even have a job, and the last time I went was three years ago. Hey, would you like to see my photos?

Vocabulary

1 Complete each sentence with a word from the box.

> beach   castle   church   fountain   hill
> office building   square   statue

a) Have you seen the _____ of Shakespeare outside the theater?

b) Let's go swimming at the _____ .

c) On Saturdays, there is a market in the large _____ in the middle of the town.

d) She works in a new _____ in the business area downtown.

e) The _____ was built in the sixteenth century to defend the city.

f) The park is on a _____ and has good views of the city.

g) They wanted to have a traditional wedding in a _____ .

h) Throw some coins into the _____ ; it will bring you good luck.

2 Search the word square (↑ ↓ → ←) for fifteen adjectives. Eight adjectives can be used to describe things you like, and seven adjectives can be used to describe things you do not like.

S	U	S	E	L	E	S	S	C	Q
P	D	U	L	L	S	G	G	I	M
E	E	Y	L	G	U	N	N	T	I
C	L	J	G	G	O	I	I	S	S
T	B	L	R	N	L	T	T	A	E
A	I	U	E	I	U	I	S	T	R
C	R	F	A	Z	B	C	U	N	A
U	R	W	T	A	A	X	G	A	B
L	E	A	X	M	F	E	S	F	L
A	T	T	R	A	C	T	I	V	E
R	Y	L	E	V	O	L	D	Z	O

things you like   *things you don't like*

spectacular   ugly

amazing   _____

lovely   _____

_____   _____

_____   _____

_____   _____

_____

3 Complete each sentence with a country adjective.

Example
A sombrero is a M<u>exican</u> hat.

a) Bordeaux is a F_____ wine.

b) Fuji is a J_____ mountain.

c) Goulash is a H_____ dish.

d) Guinness is an I_____ beer.

e) Inter Milan is an I_____ football team.

f) Lisbon is the P_____ capital.

g) The Great Pyramid is an E_____ monument.

h) The tango is an A_____ dance.

4 Complete each sentence with *in*, *on*, or *at*.

Example
The restaurants are great; _in_ fact, they're the best in the world.

a) I sometimes wish all the tourists would leave us _____ peace.

b) Many tourists come to the city to take part _____ the Mardi Gras carnival.

c) Sitges is a town _____ the coast, not far from Barcelona.

d) The best residential areas are _____ the north and west of the city.

e) The parks are all _____ the other side of the city.

f) The place is dead during the day, but it comes alive _____ night.

g) There are four prizes you could win _____ the fantastic contest.

Pronunciation

Look at the box of verbs from this unit that have two syllables. Do they have the stress on the first or the second syllable? Put them into the correct column.

> ~~decide~~   describe   discuss   ~~enter~~   explain
> happen   label   listen   mention   practice
> relax   repeat   suppose   visit

Oo   oO

enter   decide

_____   _____

_____   _____

_____   _____

_____   _____

_____   _____

Listen to the recording to check your answers.

Writing

1 Replace each underlined word or phrase in the postcard with a word or phrase from the list.

a few days ago	go in the afternoon	Mom and Dad	some interesting ruins
evening	Brasília	places of interest	take pictures
fabulous	lots	professor of archeology	terrible
food	Love	sightseeing	

Dear <u>Bill</u>,

I got here <u>last Friday</u>, and I'm having a <u>great</u> time. The weather is <u>not good</u>, but there are <u>plenty</u> of things to do. There are a few <u>cafes</u> near the hotel where I <u>play cards</u> and <u>chat with other tourists</u>. I've met a <u>nice girl</u> from <u>Madrid</u> who is taking me to a <u>great new club</u> tomorrow. The <u>nightlife</u> is interesting—so different from at home. I'm always really tired in the <u>morning</u> after so much <u>going out</u> – I'll need a vacation after this!

<u>Best wishes</u>,

Barry

2 Now write your own postcard. Replace the underlined words with words of your own choice.

3 Couples

Grammar

1 Put each verb in parentheses into the simple past.

Romeo _was_ (be) in love with Rosaline, but one day at a party he (a) _____ (meet) Juliet. He immediately (b) _____ (fall) in love with her and (c) _____ (forget) all about Rosaline. Unfortunately, Romeo's family and Juliet's family (d) _____ (be) enemies. Her family (e) _____ (want) her to marry someone else. To cut a long story short, Romeo (f) _____ (kill) himself because he (g) _____ (think) that Juliet (h) _____ (be) dead. Then, Juliet (i) _____ (wake) up and (j) _____ (find) Romeo's body. So she (k) _____ (take) Romeo's sword and (l) _____ (kill) herself, too.

2 Read the text in exercise 1 again and write questions for the following answers.

Example
Who _was Romeo in love_ with?
Rosaline.

a) Where _____ ?
At a party.

b) Who _____ about?
Rosaline.

c) Who _____ marry?
Someone else.

d) Who _____ ?
Himself.

e) Why _____ ?
Because he thought Juliet was dead.

f) What _____
when she woke up?
She killed herself, too.

g) How _____ ?
With Romeo's sword.

3 Look at the picture of a modern Romeo and Juliet. Complete each sentence with a verb from the box in the past continuous.

feel	get	hold	hope	make	sit
talk	~~wear~~				

Example
Juliet _was wearing_ an old T-shirt.

a) She _____ a cup of coffee.

b) It was late, and she _____ tired.

c) Romeo _____ on his motorcycle.

d) He _____ for a date.

e) They _____ on their cell phones.

f) A dog _____ a lot of noise.

g) Romeo _____ wet.

4 Put each verb in parentheses into the correct form. Use the simple past or the past continuous.

Juliet _was going_ (go) out with a man called Paris, but she didn't love him. One evening, she (a) _____ (watch) TV when the telephone rang. It was Romeo, and he (b) _____ (say) that he was in the street below. She (c) _____ (open) the door of the balcony and saw him in the street. He (d) _____ (sit) on a motorcycle. When he saw her, he (e) _____ (begin) to sing. It was a beautiful song, and Juliet (f) _____ (want) it to last forever. But it (g) _____ (rain), and she was cold and wet. She (h) _____ (decide) to ask Romeo inside. Then, another motorcycle (i) _____ (arrive). It was Paris…

Reading

1 Read the story about the famous opera singer Maria Callas and put the paragraphs in the correct order.

1 [B] 2 [ ] 3 [ ] 4 [ ]

2 Put the events below in the correct order.

a) He bought presents for her.
b) He died.
c) He called her.
d) Maria got married.
e) Onassis got married.
f) She died.
g) She fell in love.
h) She met Onassis.
i) She split up with her husband.
j) They had fights.
k) They went on vacation together.
l) He asked her to go out with him.

1	2	3	4	5	6	7	8	9	10	11	12
d											f

3 Answer the questions.

a) What happened when Maria was staying in Venice?

_____

_____

b) Why did Maria love Onassis?

_____

_____

c) Why did she have fights with Onassis?

_____

_____

d) How did she find out about Onassis's marriage?

_____

_____

e) Why did Onassis begin visiting Maria again?

_____

_____

f) What was Maria doing on Skorpios?

_____

_____

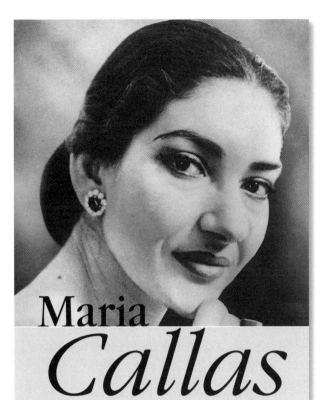

Maria *Callas*

A At the time, Maria said, "I have lost everything." After this, she stayed at home and she did not take care of herself. Two years later people could still see her on the island of Skorpios, crying next to the grave of Onassis. A little later, Maria died of a heart attack.

B Maria Callas was singing in Verona when she met the impresario Giovanni Meneghini. He became her manager, and they got married. But Maria was unhappy in the marriage, and in 1957, when she was staying in Venice, she met the Greek tycoon Aristotle Onassis. Onassis began calling her. He invited her to parties, and he bought her beautiful presents. Maria fell in love with him, and two years later, she and her husband split up.

C She saw him less and less often, and then one day in 1968 she was reading the newspaper when she saw a report about his marriage to Jackie Kennedy. It was not a happy marriage, and Onassis began to visit Maria again. Sometimes she agreed to see him; sometimes she refused. Life continued in this way for some time, but finally, in 1975, Onassis died.

D Onassis took her on vacation, and Maria told reporters that she was in love. She said that she loved him not for his money but because he was "the first man to treat me like a woman." She dreamed of marriage and wanted to have children, but after a while Onassis became tired of the relationship. He was now seeing other women, and they had fights.

Vocabulary

1 Put the lines of this love story about Frank Sinatra and Ava Gardner in the right order.

a) When Sinatra fell in

b) relationship, and when they split up, he was

c) love with Ava Gardner, he was already

d) only three years, but Ava Gardner was the love

e) married, but he couldn't resist her. He got

f) in love with her.

g) heartbroken. Their marriage lasted

h) of Frank Sinatra's life. Later, Sinatra admitted that he would always be

i) divorced so that he could marry her. It was a stormy

1	2	3	4	5	6	7	8	9
a								f

▭ Listen to the recording to check your answers.

2 Complete the text with words from the box.

affair   divorced   dream   lover
marriage   rumors   unfaithful   ~~wedding~~

In 1981, Charles, Prince of Wales, married Lady Diana Spencer. The _wedding_ was watched by millions on TV. For the British public, it was a

(a) _____ come true. But for Charles and Diana, it was never a happy

(b) _____ . Charles was

(c) _____ from the start with his

(d) _____ , Camilla Parker Bowles. After a few years, there began to be

(e) _____ about Diana, too. She had an

(f) _____ with her riding teacher. Nobody was surprised when Charles and Diana finally got (g) _____ .

3 Complete each sentence with *have* or *get*.

Example
He put his arm around her when it started to _get_ dark.

a) I'm afraid I _____ no idea what you're talking about.

b) If you ever _____ an affair with someone, I will never speak to you again.

c) Let's not _____ a fight about this; let's discuss it calmly.

d) More and more couples in Europe do not want to _____ children.

e) On their first evening together, they decided to _____ married.

f) One day, I'm going to _____ tired of all your questions.

g) They couldn't _____ divorced because of their religious beliefs.

4 Complete each phrasal verb with *out* or *up*.

Example
This is the fourth time they have split _up_ , but they always get together again later.

a) Find _____ how much money he has before you say yes!

b) He grew _____ in Mexico City, but he lives in Oaxaca now.

c) I'm much too shy to ask him _____ .

d) My boss is taking me _____ to an expensive restaurant.

e) Maybe I'll call him _____ and tell him it's over.

f) They stayed _____ all night watching romantic movies on TV.

g) They went _____ together for twelve years before getting engaged.

Pronunciation

1 ▭ Listen to the recording and circle the word that you hear.

a) began / begun

b) drank / drunk

c) ran / run

d) rang / rung

e) sang / sung

f) sank / sunk

g) swam / swum

2 Look at the word *read* in the following sentences. How is it pronounced in each sentence?

a) I read the newspaper every morning before I go to work.

b) I read *War and Peace* last year.

c) Have you read the newspaper today?

▭ Listen to the recording to check your answers.

Writing

Look at the pictures and write the story of Bonnie and Clyde. Use the questions to help you.

Begin the story like this:
Bonnie Parker was a waitress at Marco's Cafe in Rowena, Texas. One day she …

Picture 1
Who did she meet?
What was he like?
Did Bonnie and Clyde fall in love at first sight?

Picture 2
Did Bonnie wear her best clothes the next day?
Where were Bonnie and Clyde walking?
What did Clyde see?

Picture 3
Did Bonnie and Clyde steal the car?
Where did they drive after this?

Picture 4
Who did Clyde point his gun at?
What was Bonnie doing while Clyde was taking the money?

Picture 5
Where did Bonnie and Clyde go a week later?
What did they do there?

Picture 6
Where did Bonnie and Clyde go three weeks later?
Why?
What happened when a policeman tried to arrest them?

Picture 7
What were Bonnie and Clyde doing six months later?
Where were the policemen?
Who were they waiting for?

Picture 8
Who fired their guns?
Who died?

BONNIE AND CLYDE

THEY WERE YOUNG … THEY WERE IN LOVE … AND THEY KILLED PEOPLE.

4 Fit

Grammar

1 Complete each sentence with the comparative form of the adjective in parentheses.

Example
A salad is <u>healthier</u> (healthy) for you than a cheeseburger.

a) Healthy people are often _____ (happy) than people who are not fit.

b) It's _____ (hot) than yesterday, isn't it?

c) Michael Schumacher is a _____ (successful) racing driver than his brother.

d) Swimming is _____ (good) for your health than golf.

e) The nightlife in a large city is _____ (interesting) than in a small town.

f) The crowd was _____ (big) than usual, and both teams played well.

g) Your spelling is _____ (bad) than mine!

2 Solve the puzzle.

Daniel is fitter than David, but less fit than Jake. Lizzie is fitter than Daniel, but less fit than Jake. Rosa is fitter than all of them.

Put these five people in order of fitness.

the fittest   _____

                _____

                _____

                _____

the least fit   _____

3 Complete each sentence with the superlative form of an adjective from the box.

big	expensive	~~heavy~~	high	lucky
long	rich	dry		

Example
<u>The heaviest</u> animal is the blue whale, which weighs from a hundred to a hundred fifty tons.

a) _____ island in the world is Greenland (840,000 sq mi).

b) _____ woman in the world won nearly $200 million in the Massachusetts Lottery.

c) _____ waterfall in the world is the Salto Angel in Venezuela.

d) At $466 million, the Stade de France was _____ stadium in the world when it was built.

e) From 1964 to 2001, the Atacama Desert was _____ place in the world.

f) The Sumitomo Bank is _____ in the world.

g) The Andes mountain range is _____ in the world.

4 There is one word missing from each line in the text below. Insert the missing words. Choose from the words in the box. You can use them more than once.

as	more	most	not	than	the

        most

Probably the⁄common health problem for men is heart disease. Exercise is important, but not important as a healthy diet. A bad diet is biggest cause of this disease. Vegetables are better for you fatty foods, but some vegetables are useful than others. Supermarket products are as healthy as organic produce. People with most stressful jobs have shorter lives people who are stress-free, so look for ways to relax. You should exercise more once a week. A hard, sweaty sport is not good for you regular, gentle exercise.

Listening and reading

1 📼 Cover the tapescript opposite and listen to part of a TV program about sports. Match the sports in the pictures to the three stories.

2 📼 Listen to the program again. Which sports personalities are the following sentences talking about? Write your answers in the boxes:
SK—Shinzo Kanaguri; EM—Eric Moussambani;
EE—Eddie Edwards.

a) He came from Britain. ☐

b) He didn't enjoy taking part in his race. ☐

c) He needed to wear glasses. ☐

d) He took part in the Sydney Olympics. ☐

e) He stopped in the middle of the race. ☐

f) He only started the sport that year. ☐

g) He took part in the Stockholm Olympics. ☐

h) He broke some bones. ☐

i) He broke an Olympic record. ☐

j) They had a problem with the weather. ☐
   ☐

3 Look at the tapescript and choose the best definition of each word below, a) or b).

1 competitors (*line 7*)
   a) people taking part in a race
   b) people watching a race

2 blazing (*line 9*)
   a) very hot b) very cold

3 disqualified (*line 22*)
   a) allowed to continue
   b) not allowed to continue

4 jaw (*line 43*)
   a) a bone of the face b) a record

5 drops (*line 49*)
   a) jumps b) falls

6 nearsighted (*line 54*)
   a) can see well b) can't see well

Today we take a look at three of the greatest losers in the history of the Olympic Games. The first one was a certain Shinzo Kanaguri from Japan. He
5 ran in the 1912 Olympics in Stockholm— the marathon. It was an extremely hot day, and like all the other competitors, Shinzo was finding it extremely hard. As he was running along under the blazing
10 sun, he saw a family sitting on the side of the road, having a picnic. They invited him to join them for their meal. After eating, he realized that there was little point in continuing the race.

15 Number two is Eric Moussambani, also known as Eric the Eel. At the Sydney Olympics, Eric set a new Olympic record in the 100-meter freestyle. He won his race in the record slow time of 1 minute
20 52.72 seconds. There were two other swimmers in the race, but both of them were disqualified for false starts. Although he won the race, Eric's time was too slow to qualify for the final. His
25 time was just a little slower than the Olympic champion, Pieter van den Hoogenband, but van den Hoogenband swam 200 meters, compared to Eric's 100. Eric was just happy to finish his race
30 —it was his first time in a 50-meter pool, and he had only taken up swimming a few months before.

My number three is Britain's very own sports superstar, Eddie Edwards—Eddie
35 the Eagle. Eddie's chosen sport was a strange choice for a man who lives hundreds of miles from the nearest mountain. But at the Winter Olympics in Calgary, Eddie was the only member of
40 the British ski-jumping team, and he was entered for both the 70- and the 90- meter jumps. While he was preparing for the Olympics, he broke his jaw, his collarbone, and a number of teeth. But
45 at Calgary, Eddie was ready—and came in last in the 70-meter event. The Olympic officials did not want him to take part in the longer jump. "The Eagle doesn't jump—he drops like a stone,"
50 said one Olympic official. But Eddie insisted and, once more, took last place —forty-seven meters behind the winner. At least he had a good excuse. Eddie the Eagle was very nearsighted and wore
55 thick glasses. In the cold mountain air, Eddie's glasses misted up, and he couldn't see a thing.

Vocabulary

1 Complete the chart. Use a dictionary if necessary.

sport	person	place
a) _____	boxer	ring
swimming	b) _____	pool
gymnastics	c) _____	gym
ice hockey	d) _____	rink
rowing	e) _____	river/lake
f) _____	skier	slope
g) _____	racquetball player	court

2 Fill each blank with *does*, *plays*, or *goes*.

Mike is a fitness freak. First thing in the morning, he either _goes_ for a run or (a) _____ swimming at the local pool. When he gets back, he (b) _____ the housework, and then sets off for his job at the gym. It's the perfect job, because he (c) _____ weight training and other exercises during his breaks. Three evenings a week, he (d) _____ racquetball with his best friend, and twice a week he (e) _____ karate. On Fridays he (f) _____ dancing with his friends from the gym. On Saturdays, he (g) _____ shopping in the morning, but in the afternoon he (h) _____ on a neighborhood football team. During vacations, he usually (i) _____ windsurfing. It is, he says, the only way to stay beautiful.

3 Replace each underlined word with a word from the box.

attractive	average	calm	famous	fit
fortunate	fun	~~unhappy~~		

Example
Are you <u>sad</u> when your team loses a football game? *unhappy*

a) Are some gold medal winners at the Olympics very <u>lucky</u>?

b) Are the best tennis players always <u>cool</u> before a match?

c) Do you know any <u>good-looking</u> boxers?

d) Do you need to be <u>healthy</u> to play golf?

e) How much does the <u>typical</u> football player earn?

f) Which do you think are more <u>enjoyable</u>: team sports or individual sports?

g) Who is the most <u>well-known</u> sports personality in your country?

4 Make adjectives from the nouns in the box. Use the adjectives to complete the sentences.

aerobics	danger	~~interest~~	profession
success	sweat	talent	value

Example
Baseball is the least <u>interesting</u> sport in the world: nothing ever happens!

a) _____ basketball players can earn millions of dollars.

b) He's always very _____ after the game, so he takes a shower.

c) It's important to do _____ exercises to keep fit.

d) Auto racing is a lot more _____ than golf.

e) Only the most _____ athletes win medals at the Olympics.

f) The New York Yankees are probably the most _____ baseball team of all time.

g) Some soccer players' feet are extremely _____: they are insured for millions.

5 Match the phrases in box A with the words in box B to complete the expressions.

A

a) He was as cold as
b) His face was as white as
c) He is as strong as
d) My face was as red as
e) She's as brave as
f) The children were as good as
g) She was as quiet as

B

1 a beet
2 a mouse
3 a sheet
4 a lion
5 gold
6 ice
7 an ox

Writing

1 Rewrite the story below, using correct punctuation. You will need ten capital letters and ten periods.

a man was feeling sick, and he went to see the doctor he went with his wife because he was a little worried afterwards the doctor spoke to the man's wife he said, "I'm afraid I have some bad news unless you follow my instructions very carefully, your husband will die every morning you must give him a good breakfast, and you must cook him a healthy meal at night what's more, you must not ask him to do any housework, and you must keep the house very clean it is a lot of work for you, but it really is the only way to keep him alive"

on the way home, the husband asked his wife what the doctor had said to her "he said you're going to die," she replied

2 Correct the spelling mistakes in the story below.

One day a buss driver was in his buss when the bigest man he had ever seen got on. The giant looked at the driver, said, "Big John dosn't pay," and took his seet on the buss. The buss driver was only a litle man, and he did not want to argue.

The next day, the same thing hapened. The man mountain got on the buss, looked at the driver, and said, "Big John dosn't pay." Then he went to a seet.

This hapened for sevral days. After a weak, the driver was begining to get a litle angry. Evrybody else payed, so why not the big man? So the driver went to a gym and began a course of bodybilding. He did not want to be frihgtened of Big John anymore.

Two weaks later, the driver had strong mussles and was feelling very fit. At the usual stopp, Big John got on. "Big John dosn't pay," he said. But this time the driver was preppared for him. He got up and said, "Oh, yeah? And why dosn't Big John pay?"

The man reached into his poket. For a momment, the driver was extremely scared. Perrhaps he had a gun. Then the man replyed, "Becase Big John has a buss pass."

Pronunciation

1 How do you say the following numbers?

1 $63 million
   a) sixty-three million dollars
   b) sixty-three millions dollars
   c) dollars sixty-three million

2 47.75 mi
   a) forty-seven point seventy-five mile
   b) forty-seven point seven five miles
   c) forty-seven comma seventy-five miles

3 6.6%
   a) six comma six percent
   b) six point six percent
   c) six comma six percents

4 110 mph
   a) a hundred ten mile an hour
   b) a hundred ten an hour
   c) a hundred ten miles an hour

5 13–0 (football)
   a) thirteen and nothing
   b) thirteen nothing c) thirteen for nothing

6 2 ¾
   a) two and three four
   b) two and three quarter
   c) two and three quarters

7 0.675
   a) zero point six seven five
   b) zero point six hundred seventy five
   c) zero point sixty-seven five

🔲 Listen to the recording to check your answers.

2 The words below all have three syllables. Do they have the stress on the first or the second syllable? Put them into the correct columns.

advertise   attractive   certainly
cheeseburger   marathon   opinion
percentage   photograph   statistics
surprising   tournament   wonderful

Ooo   oOo
advertise   attractive
_____   _____
_____   _____
_____   _____
_____   _____
_____   _____

🔲 Listen to the recording to check your answers.

5 *Review 1*

Grammar

1 Put each word in the box into one of the three categories (*verbs*, *nouns*, or *adjectives*) in column A. Then complete column B.

~~bad~~	~~beach~~	~~become~~	catch	child
choose	church	draw	fall	fight
foot	friendly	lucky	meet	mouse
pay	sad	send	shy	thin	tooth
ugly	university	wet	win	

A	**B**
verbs	*past tense*
become	became
_____	_____
_____	_____
_____	_____
_____	_____
_____	_____
_____	_____
_____	_____
_____	_____
_____	_____
nouns	*plural*
beach	beaches
_____	_____
_____	_____
_____	_____
_____	_____
_____	_____
adjectives	*comparative*
bad	worse
_____	_____
_____	_____
_____	_____
_____	_____
_____	_____
_____	_____

2 Rearrange the words to make questions.

Example
any children have Do you ?
Do you have any children?

a) best did friend meet When you your ?

_____

b) class in is person tallest the Who your ?

_____

c) country in is like the weather What your ?

_____

d) day do e-mails every get How many you ?

_____

e) does teacher like look What your ?

_____

f) wearing were What yesterday you ?

_____

3 Each of the sentences below has *one* word missing. Insert the missing word.

Example   do
What names/you like for a boy?

a) He drinks far much beer.

b) How your parents choose your name?

c) It raining when I arrived at work.

d) There were lot of people at the party.

e) Tiger Woods is greatest golfer of all time.

f) Venus Williams isn't as tall Shaquille O'Neal.

g) What the stores like in your hometown?

4 Circle the best alternative.

"Wake up, darling, it's a beautiful morning," said Mrs. Everest.

"Ughh," replied her husband. "Why ~~did you wake~~/ *woke you* me? I (a) *slept/was sleeping*."

"It's (b) *more/the most* beautiful day of the year. Why (c) *don't we go/we not go* to the country and get some fresh (d) *air/airs*? If we leave now, there won't be (e) *much / many* traffic."

A (f) *few/little* hours later, Mr. Everest was finally ready. They (g) *got/were getting* into the car and set off. At twelve o'clock, they (h) *drove/were driving* along a country road when Mr. Everest (i) *saw/was seeing* a country restaurant. "That (j) *looks/looks like* nice. Why (k) *don't we/we don't* stop there for lunch?"

After a long lunch, they (l) *got/were getting* back into the car and (m) *continued/were continuing* their journey. After another hour, Mrs. Everest (n) *turned/was turning* to her husband and (o) *said/was saying* nervously, "Darling, I think I (p) *left/was leaving* my handbag in the restaurant." Her husband (q) *looked/looked like* really angry. "Typical, typical…," he said under his breath. When (r) *did they get/they got* back to the restaurant, he was still angry. "It's already four o'clock," he said. "We don't have (s) *enough time/time enough* to go to the country now. What a waste of time!" Mrs. Everest got out of the car and was walking toward the restaurant when her husband (t) *stopped/was stopping* her.

"I almost forgot. (u) *Can you ask/Do you can ask* them if they have my hat?"

5 Rewrite the sentences, beginning with the words given.

Example
We have no children.
We don't have any children.

a) What's your weight?
How much _____

b) There were only a few people at the party.
There were not _____

c) I didn't get much sleep last night.
I didn't get a _____

d) She has known him for two years.
She met _____

e) What clothes did you have on yesterday?
What were _____

f) Michael isn't as attractive as Raúl.
Raúl is _____

g) Cathy is older than Tom.
Tom isn't _____

h) There isn't a golfer in the world who is better than Tiger Woods.
Tiger Woods is the _____

6 Find a response in box B to each sentence in box A.

A

a) Are you interested in football?
b) How long does it take you to do your homework?
c) How often do you go to the gym?
d) Is there anything you don't like about your job?
e) What do you have in common with your sister?
f) What's up? Are you all right?
g) What's your favorite song by Celine Dion?
h) What's your new teacher like?

B

1 Not really. I split up with my boyfriend last night.
2 Everything! She even looks like me.
3 It depends. Sometimes a half an hour, sometimes longer.
4 No, not at all. I think it's perfect.
5 Not really. I've never been to a game in my life.
6 Oh, once or twice a week usually.
7 She's lovely, and her classes are fantastic.
8 Who? Never heard of her!

Vocabulary

1 Look at the picture and say if the sentences are true (T) or false (F).

Example

Two people are sightseeing and taking

pictures. ☐T

a) The man and woman are middle-aged. ☐

b) They are having a fight. ☐

c) The woman is standing in front of a statue. ☐

d) She has blond hair and a big smile. ☐

e) There is a cafe on the other side of the canal. ☐

f) The cafe does not have a good view of the canal because of the traffic. ☐

g) A nurse in uniform is sitting at the cafe. ☐

h) There is an old bridge over the canal. ☐

i) A man in a boat is using his cell phone. ☐

j) He does not look very fit. ☐

k) There is a castle next to the cafe. ☐

l) Most of the architecture of the town is very modern. ☐

2 Complete each sentence with *down, out,* or *up.*

Example

We need to find <u>out</u> what time the train leaves.

a) He's completely stressed _____ about his new job.

b) I think it's so romantic that he gave _____ his throne for the woman he loved.

c) I think I'll stay _____ and watch the late night movie on TV.

d) I thought you were never going to ask me _____ .

e) Listen carefully and write _____ the words you hear.

f) She was born and grew _____ in the south of Egypt.

g) They split _____ when he met someone else.

h) Why don't you call me _____ tonight and we'll talk about it?

3 Put the missing words in the grid below to find the hidden words in the gray boxes.

Example

He was so......! I've never seen anyone so unattractive!

a) The children were really ...... —we couldn't hear ourselves speak.

b) I need to ...... my English—it's not good enough.

c) The runners were on the ......, waiting for the race to begin.

d) The senator died yesterday, and his ...... will be next week.

e) When did Alexander Bell ...... the telephone?

f) They live in a small ...... with a population of about a hundred people.

g) In her new job, she will ...... about sixty thousand dollars a year.

	U	G	L	Y	
a)		O		Y	
b)		M			E
c)		R		K	
d)		U			L
e)		N		T	
f)		I			E
g)		A	N		

4 Circle the best alternative.

Example
Does he ever *get/have/make* tired of talking?

a) Do you *get/have/make* a lot in common with your sister?
b) I *get/have/make* no idea what you are talking about.
c) I think he's *getting/having/making* an affair with his secretary.
d) I'm tired—let's *get/have/make* a taxi.
e) It's time to *get/have/make* a decision—what do you think?
f) They *got/had/made* married just after they graduated.
g) What time does it *get/have/make* dark in August?
h) You can improve your memory if you learn to *get/have/make* different associations.
i) You have to *get/have/make* a choice—it's your work or me!

5 Make nouns from the following words.

Example
choose   *choice*

a) dangerous   _____
b) decide   _____
c) describe   _____
d) fashionable   _____
e) introduce   _____
f) lucky   _____
g) marry   _____
h) noisy   _____
i) operate   _____
j) religious   _____
k) romantic   _____
l) succeed   _____

6 Complete each sentence with a noun from exercise 5.

Example
Good luck on your exam tomorrow.

a) Can you give us a _____ of the person who stole your money?
b) For the first course, you have a _____ between soup and salad.
c) He had to go to the hospital for an _____ on his back.
d) His first movie was a great _____ and won four Oscars.
e) People who drink and drive are a _____ to other drivers.

f) They had an unhappy _____ and separated after a few years.
g) What color is in _____ this summer?
h) Your written homework needs an _____ , a middle, and a conclusion.

7 Replace the words in *italics* with their opposites from the box and rewrite the story. You may need to change *a* to *an.*

boring	cheap	difficult	least	poor
terrible	unattractive	~~unusual~~	worst	

I went out on a *typical* date with my boyfriend yesterday. He took me to a very *expensive* restaurant, and I had the *best* meal of my life. The food was *fantastic,* and the wine was the *most* expensive on the menu. John is an *easy* man to be with: he's *rich* and *good-looking,* and he can be very *amusing.* When he asked me to marry him, I said…

I went out on an unusual date with … .

_____
_____
_____
_____
_____
_____
_____
_____
_____
_____

8 Find and correct the twelve spelling mistakes in the story below.

One day, a man didn't come home from work. The next morning he still wasn't there, so his wife went to the police. They asked her to describe her husbend's apearance. "He's 38, avrage hieght, he's extreemly good-looking, with a mustashe, dark hair, athletic build, and he looks very inteligent."

Later in the day, her freind said, "Why did you say that? He's the compleat oposite. He's very short, overwieght, and has a face like a cheesburger!"

"I know," said the wife, "but I don't want the police to bring *him* back."

husband's _____ _____

_____ _____ _____

_____ _____ _____

_____ _____ _____

6 *Shop*

Grammar

1 Complete each sentence with *for* or *to*.

Example
I think I'll buy some perfume _for_ my grandmother.

a) I told your secret _____ *my husband*—I hope that's O.K.

b) I lent my car _____ *my sister*.

c) Philip made a delicious dinner _____ *his girlfriend*.

d) Why don't you get some candy _____ *your mother*?

e) You need to show your bus pass _____ *the driver*.

f) Give the ticket _____ *the receptionist*.

g) I sent a letter _____ *the company president* last week.

2 Rewrite the sentences in exercise 1. Replace the words in *italics* with a pronoun (*him* or *her*) and do not use *for* or *to*.

Example
I think I'll buy her some perfume.

a) _____
b) _____
c) _____
d) _____
e) _____
f) _____
g) _____

3 Some of the sentences below contain a word that should not be there. Cross out the unnecessary words. Four sentences are correct.

Example
She told ~~to~~ me all about her new job.

a) I'm going to write a letter to you very soon.

b) She sent the tickets to the wrong address.

c) I gave for my nephew a gold pen for his birthday.

d) We've brought to you some really good news.

e) He is teaching history to college students this year.

f) Can I show my pictures to you one day?

g) The salesclerk explained me the advantages of speed dialing.

h) She described us the new leopard-skin miniskirt she had bought.

4 Rearrange the words to make sentences.

Example
a always diet is on She
She is always on a diet.

a) drives He crazy me often
_____

b) ever hardly I perfume wear
_____

c) arrive doesn't She on time usually
_____

d) a been center garden have I never to
_____

e) about her husband is positive rarely She
_____

f) celebrate Day don't We often Valentine's
_____

g) at presents good I'm normally not choosing very
_____

5 Complete each sentence with an appropriate form of the verb in parentheses.

Example
He really hates _getting up_ (get up) in the morning.

a) He often decides _____ (stay) in bed all day.

b) He enjoys _____ (spend) the evening in front of the TV.

c) He wastes hours _____ (surf) the net.

d) He doesn't mind _____ (eat) junk food every day.

e) He doesn't need _____ (look) for a job.

f) He wants _____ (have) a life of leisure.

g) He spends his summers _____ (go) to free festivals.

Reading

1 Look at the newspaper article opposite. The article contains a mistake. One sentence does not belong. Find the sentence and cross it out.

2 Choose the best answer.

1 What is special about the store Out of the Closet?
  a) It is in London's fashionable Bond Street.
  b) All the clothes are of very high quality.
  c) The clothes are all old.
  d) All the clothes in it belonged to Elton John.

2 Why is Elton John selling his old clothes?
  a) Because he doesn't like them anymore.
  b) Because he wants to raise money for a charity.
  c) Because his closet is too small.
  d) Because his closet is empty.

3 Why did Elton John spend so much money?
  a) Because he was growing up.
  b) Because he was living in Britain.
  c) Because he was a shopaholic.
  d) Because he bought a lot of flowers.

4 What kind of people suffer most from oniomania?
  a) Americans.
  b) Pop stars.
  c) Women.
  d) Psychologists.

5 Why is oniomania more of a problem now than in the past?
  a) Because Elton John is very popular.
  b) Because psychologists have known about the problem for a long time.
  c) Because there are more stores and it is easy to get credit.
  d) Because there are more and more alcoholics and drug addicts.

6 Why do some scientists think that people are shopaholics?
  a) Because they get expensive presents instead of love when they are young.
  b) Because they spend too much time with their parents.
  c) Because they have taken antidepressant drugs.
  d) Because they don't have any scissors.

Shop Till You Drop

On Wednesday of next week, shoppers in London's fashionable Bond Street will be able to buy something special. Wednesday sees the opening of Out of the Closet, a clothing store with a difference. All the items for sale are of the highest quality: beautiful silk shirts, Versace sweaters, crocodile-skin shoes … But what makes these clothes so special is that they belonged to Elton John. He is selling his old clothes to raise money for a charity that helps AIDS victims. But even when everything has been sold, his closet will not be empty. Elton John is one of the growing number of "shopaholics" in Britain. One year he spent $37.5 million, including $450,000 on flowers and $13.5 million on property.

It is estimated that 15 million people in the U.S. suffer from the same problem as Elton John. The technical name for this disorder is "oniomania," and nine out of ten sufferers are women.

Psychologists have known about the problem for a long time. But the opening of more and more shopping malls and the easy availability of credit cards have changed everything. It's often a good idea to try on one or two pairs. There are now more shopaholics than alcoholics or drug addicts in the UK. Many have serious financial problems, but the condition also results in family breakups, homelessness, and suicide.

Scientists are trying to find out why some people enjoy shopping so much. One idea is that it is connected to problems during childhood. Many parents do not have much time to spend with their children. Instead of giving them love and affection, they buy their children expensive presents, and the child associates shopping with security and pleasure.

Fortunately, there are cures for the condition. Many people feel better when they spend money, but psychotherapy can help shopaholics discover why they are unhappy in the first place. For others, antidepressant drugs may help. But the best cure is probably to take your credit cards out of your wallet and cut them up. Remember: one pair of scissors is enough.

Vocabulary

1 Combine a word from box A with a word from box B to make a compound noun. Then use the words to complete the sentences below.

A

~~birthday~~
cell
electronic
engagement
shopping
price
clothing
evening

B

store
bag
gown
gadget
~~present~~
ring
phones
tag

Example

For my <u>birthday present</u> last year, Aunt Susan gave me a pair of socks.

a) I'm going to a formal dinner next week, and I need to buy a new _____ .

b) It was a diamond _____ , and she couldn't understand where he had found the money to buy it.

c) The _____ broke, and the bottle fell out and smashed on the floor.

d) The new _____ at the mall didn't have anything I wanted to buy.

e) Nokia is one of the best-known makers of _____ .

f) These pants normally cost $60, but the _____ was wrong, and I only had to pay $35.

g) My father always wants to buy the latest _____ .

2 Put each of the following words under the correct heading.

~~check~~	~~cotton~~	denim	leather
patterned	plain	silk	striped
synthetic	wool		

material	*pattern*
cotton	check
_____	_____
_____	_____
_____	_____
_____	_____

3 Label the pictures. The first letter of each word has been given to you.

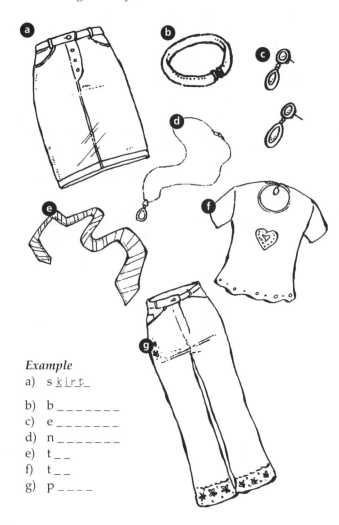

Example

a) s <u>k i r t</u>

b) b _ _ _ _ _ _ _

c) e _ _ _ _ _ _ _

d) n _ _ _ _ _ _ _

e) t _ _

f) t _ _

g) p _ _ _ _

4 Match the questions in box A with their answers in box B.

A

a) Can I have a refund if my wife doesn't like it?
b) Can I help you, ma'am?
c) Did you give me the receipt?
d) Do you take credit cards?
e) Do you think I look good in this dress?
f) Do you have anything more brightly colored?
g) Is it the right size, ma'am?
h) Would you like to try on something else?

B

1 No, but we have this nice blue one.
2 No, but you can always exchange it.
3 No, I'm sorry—here you are.
4 No, I'm sorry—just cash or checks.
5 No, it doesn't fit at all!
6 No, thanks. I'll take this one.
7 No, thanks. I'm just looking.
8 No, you look like a sack of potatoes.

Writing

Fill in the online registration form for an online shopping service.

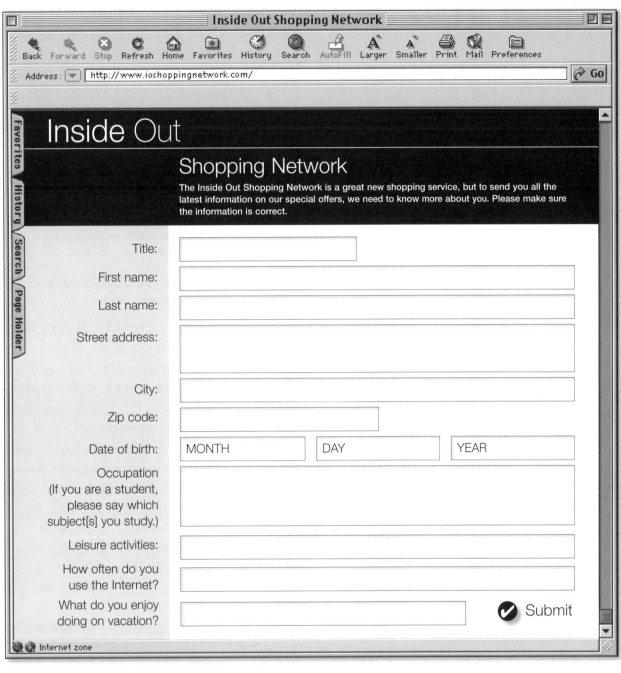

Pronunciation

Write these numbers in words.

Example

285,750

Two hundred eighty five thousand seven hundred fifty

a) 925

_____

b) 2,940

_____

c) 13,822

_____

d) 118,750

_____

e) 2,750,605

_____

f) 50,000,429

_____

g) 999,999,999

_____

Listen to the recording to check your answers.

7 Job

Grammar

1 Complete the chart. Use your dictionary if you need help.

simple verb form	simple past	past participle
break	_____	_____
cut	_____	_____
drop	_____	_____
hold	_____	_____
know	_____	_____
leave	_____	_____
pay	_____	_____
run	_____	_____
see	_____	_____
stand	_____	_____
tell	_____	_____
travel	_____	_____
try	_____	_____

2 Put the verbs into the present perfect tense.

Example
How many different jobs has she had (she have)?

a) She _____ (have) dozens of jobs in her life.

b) _____ (you ever work) in a factory?

c) No, I _____ (never be) in a factory.

d) What's the worst thing that _____ _____ (ever happen) to you in a job?

e) I _____ (hate) most of my jobs, and I hate this one, too.

f) _____ (you ever think) of running your own business?

g) Yes, I _____ (always want) to be my own boss.

3 Circle the best time expression.

Example
Did you learn to drive (when you were 18) / ever / in your life ?

a) Have you been to the movies *a few weeks ago / last week / this week* ?

b) I bought a great CD *in my life / over the years / yesterday.*

c) I didn't go to the beach at all *last summer / over the years / recently.*

d) So far, I've been to a restaurant twice *last Friday / never / this week.*

e) I've done a lot of silly things *a few years ago / last year / over the years.*

f) I've met a lot of interesting people *last year / recently / when I was a student.*

g) I've spent far too much money *last night / today / yesterday.*

4 Put each verb in parentheses into either the simple past or the present perfect.

I *have had* (have) lots of horrible jobs in my life, but the worst job I (a) _____ (ever have) was selling hot dogs. I (b) _____ (always be) a vegetarian, and I (c) _____ (never eat) a hot dog in my life. And I never will!
I (d) _____ (start) the job two years ago at the beginning of summer vacation because I (e) _____ (need) the money to pay for my classes. We (f) _____ (have) to sell the hotdogs from little carts on Sixth Avenue in New York. I (g) _____ (think) I would like the job, because I (h) _____ (always like) working outdoors. I was so wrong!
I (i) _____ (never make) such a big mistake in my whole life. The hotdogs and the onions (j) _____ (smell) disgusting, the customers (k) _____ (be) rude, and we (l) _____ (often have) problems with the police. The boss (m) _____ (be) a big, fat man in a leather jacket. He (n) _____ (shout) at us all the time. "How many (o) _____ _____ (you sell) today? You (p) _____ _____ (not sell) enough!" One day, the police (q) _____ (arrest) him, and that (r) _____ (be) the end of the job.

Listening

1 Cover the tapescripts opposite and listen to two people playing a game. One person thinks of a job and the other person has to guess what it is. Check (✓) the two jobs that are described.

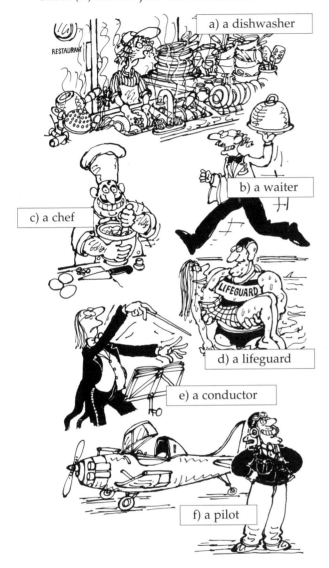

a) a dishwasher

b) a waiter

c) a chef

d) a lifeguard

e) a conductor

f) a pilot

2 Listen to the people playing the game a third time. They ask the same questions as in the first game, but the answers are different. Write down the answers (*Yes* or *No*) as you listen.

a) Do you work indoors?
b) Do you use your hands in this job?
c) Is it a well-paid job?
d) Do you need any special training for this job?
e) What hours do you work? No, wait, do you work normal office hours?
f) Do you have to work in the evenings?
g) Do you have to wear a uniform?
h) Is it a hot and smelly job?
i) I think I've got it. Do you work in a restaurant?
j) I know. You're a waiter!
k) O.K., so you're a chef?

3 Look at the pictures again. Which job is being described?

A: So, do you work indoors or outdoors?
B: I can only say "yes" or "no."
A: O.K., do you work indoors?
B: Yes.
A: Do you use your hands for this job?
B: Yes.
A: Is it a well-paying job?
B: Uhm, no, usually not.
A: Do you need any special training for this job?
B: Yes. Usually.
A: What hours do you work? No, wait, do you work normal office hours?
B: No.
A: Do you have to work at night?
B: Yes.
A: Do you have to wear a uniform?
B: Yes.
A: Is it a hot and smelly job?
B: Uh, yes, I guess so.
A: I think I've got it. Do you work in a restaurant?
B: Yes.
A: I know. You're a waiter!
B: No!
A: O.K., so you're a chef?
B: Yes, you've got it.

B: O.K., my turn. Is it a job for men or women? I mean, do men usually have this job?
A: Yes, men, usually.
B: Do you have to be strong?
A: No! Not at all.
B: Do you need any special tools?
A: Yes, one. One special tool. A kind of tool, I guess.
B: Do you work in an office?
A: No.
B: Is it an artistic job?
A: Yes.
B: Do you work in a studio?
A: Yes, sometimes.
B: Painter!
A: No.
B: Oh. Uh, I don't know. Do you travel a lot for this job?
A: Quite a lot.
B: A pilot? No, no, that's not artistic. Do you wear a uniform?
A: Yes, kind of. Special clothes.
B: Oh, I don't know. Is it something to do with music?
A: Yes!
B: Do you play an instrument?
A: No.
B: Are you a—you know—a conductor?
A: Yes. Finally!

Vocabulary

1 Search the word square (↑ ↓ → ← ↖ ↗ ↘ ↙) for seventeen jobs.

R	R	C	R	E	H	C	A	E	T	Y	P
W	E	O	H	N	D	Q	U	T	N	R	Y
A	U	H	T	E	Y	J	E	N	E	O	R
I	T	X	P	C	F	V	A	S	F	R	A
T	S	B	A	A	A	N	S	R	A	E	T
R	I	D	B	S	R	E	R	D	R	K	E
E	T	L	K	T	R	G	N	R	M	N	R
S	R	Y	O	D	T	F	O	U	E	A	C
S	A	L	R	J	U	C	N	T	R	B	E
R	I	I	R	O	T	C	O	D	O	S	S
P	A	M	I	D	W	I	F	E	Y	H	E
H	T	N	A	T	N	U	O	C	C	A	P

accountant   _____

artist   _____

_____   _____

_____   _____

_____   _____

_____   _____

_____   _____

_____

2 Complete each sentence with a word from the box.

> application   career   company   employee
> living   resignation   salary   staff

a) He wanted to have a _____ in the police force, but he failed the entrance exam.

b) I don't want to be an _____ anymore. I want to work for myself.

c) Most of the _____ members in the restaurant are unhappy with their pay.

d) She handed in her _____ , and she's leaving in four weeks.

e) The job is really interesting, but the _____ is terrible.

f) What does he do for a _____ ? He's a secret agent!

g) What kind of _____ do you work for?

h) When we receive your _____ , we will contact you for an interview.

3 Find a response in box B to each sentence in box A.

A

> a) Look at this book I just got.
> b) O.K., do exercises 1, 2, 3, 5, 7, 8, and 9 for homework.
> c) The children are going to stay with their grandparents next week.
> d) How do you change a diaper? I've never done it before.
> e) I have a problem with my computer.
> f) My job is really boring.

B

> 1 Yes, but on the other hand, it pays well.
> 2 So, you'll have a lot of time on your hands?
> 3 Well, you'll have to get a pen and paper and do it by hand!
> 4 Is it new or secondhand?
> 5 Do we hand it in tomorrow?
> 6 Would you like me to give you a hand?

4 Complete each question with a past participle. Some letters have been given to you.

Example
Do you know any teenagers who have r u n their own business?

a) Have you ever b r _ _ _ _ the law?

b) Have you ever g i _ _ _ a speech in front of a large group of people?

c) Have you ever w o _ _ _ _ nights?

d) How many days off have you h _ _ in the last six months?

e) How much money have you e a _ _ _ _ this year?

f) What's the worst restaurant you've ever e _ _ _ _ in?

g) What's the worst thing that has ever h a _ _ _ _ _ to you?

Pronunciation

🔲 Look at the text below. Practice reading it while you listen to the recording.

Hi. //
My name's Frank, //
and I come from / Jalisco / in Mexico. //
I work‿as‿an artist for‿an on-line language school, //but I also teach Spanish and English. //
I've been with the company for‿a couple‿of years, //and I enjoy my work. //

Writing

1 Look at the advertisement below and put the parts of the letter in the correct places.

New York Job Placements

Work in New York during your summer vacation

We are looking for hundreds of people for temporary jobs in New York: restaurant staff, salesclerks, office workers, nannies, summer camp counselors, travel guide editors, construction workers...

Good pay and help with accommodations provided.

Send us a short letter, telling us

a when you are available for work,

b what work experience you have, enclosing a résumé, and

c what kind of work you prefer.

Send to: Sandra Evans, New York Job Placements, P.O. Box 414B, New York, NY 10099

a) July 6, 2003

b) I am writing in reply to your advertisement in *International Travel Monthly.*

c) I am a third-year engineering student at the University of the Americas in Puebla.

d) I am available for work this summer in the months of July and August.

e) Please see my résumé for further details.

f) Yours sincerely,

g) I have experience working in restaurants and offices. I have also worked with children.

h) *Carlos Vega*

i) Av. 14 Poniente, 2567
Puebla
Mexico

j) I look forward to hearing from you.

k) I would prefer a job where I could practice my English, but I would be happy to consider any offer.

l) Carlos Vega

m) Dear Ms. Evans,

n) Sandra Evans
New York Job Placements
P.O. Box 414B
New York, NY 10099

1 i	
2	**3**
4	
5	
6, 7	
8, 9, 10	
11	
12	
13	
14	

2 Use the letter above as a model and write your own reply to the advertisement.

8 *Rich*

Grammar

1 Correct the grammatical mistake in each sentence.

Example

What ~~we are~~ *are we* going to do tonight, Veronica?

a) I'm tired. I going to have an early night.

b) What about tomorrow? Are you go to be free in the evening?

c) Yes, but I not am going to go out. I want to watch TV.

d) Are you going come with me to my parents' house on Saturday?

e) No, I'm going to seeing Tony and Carla this weekend.

f) Veronica, when are we going get married?

g) I've already told you, Barry. We're never to going get married.

2 Look at each sentence below. Does the present continuous refer to the present (P) or to the future (F)?

Example

Are you enjoying your English classes? *F*

a) State governors are meeting in Atlanta on Friday.

b) He's doing three concerts in Los Angeles and two in San Francisco.

c) I'm feeling really great, thank you.

d) She's getting a lot of attention because of her new album.

e) They're moving into their new house this weekend.

f) This is John Rivera of ABC News, and I'm speaking from Rio de Janeiro.

g) We're having a party on Saturday. Would you like to come?

3 Look at Matt McKay's list of appointments for Tuesday and write sentences, using the present continuous. Use the verbs in the box.

attend	fly	give	have	~~meet~~

TUESDAY

10 a.m.	Lawyer
1 p.m.	Lunch with Mom
3 p.m.	Interview (MTV studios)
6 p.m.	JFK Airport—Los Angeles
8 p.m.	American Music Awards ceremony

Example

He's meeting his lawyer at 10 o'clock.

a) _____

b) _____

c) _____

d) _____

4 Rearrange the words to make questions. Then answer the questions.

Example

are bed go going time to to tonight What you ?
What time are you going to go to bed tonight?
Answer: *I'm going to go to bed at midnight.*

a) are for going have lunch to tomorrow What you ?

_____

_____

Answer: _____

_____

b) after are do going school to What you ?

_____

_____

Answer: _____

_____

c) are do going this to weekend What you ?

_____

_____

Answer: _____

_____

Reading

1 Choose the best headline for the newspaper article opposite.

- **Getty Becomes British**
- **Getty Helps Troubled Conservative Party**
- **Getty's Son Kidnapped by Mafia**
- **National Gallery Gets £50 Million**

2 Read the article again and decide if the following sentences are true (T) or false (F).

a) Getty often donates money to political parties. ☐

b) Getty's father made his money from oil. ☐

c) The Conservative Party has recently changed its leader. ☐

d) Getty doesn't like the British way of life. ☐

e) Getty gave £50 million to the British Film Institute. ☐

f) Last year, he gave £1 million to a homeless drug addict. ☐

g) His last wife died of drugs. ☐

h) Getty cut his son's ear off. ☐

i) Getty became religious later in his life. ☐

j) The British government was Conservative when the article was written. ☐

3 Complete the sentences below with words from the article opposite. The first letter of each word has been given to you.

a) Who did you vote for in the last presidential e_____ ? (*paragraph 1*)

b) Have you ever d_____ anything to charity? (*paragraph 1*)

c) I am very g_____ to my parents for helping me in so many ways. (*paragraph 1*)

d) It's a special hospital that takes care of drug a_____ and alcoholics. (*paragraph 2*)

e) Terrorists have k_____ the son of the President and are asking for $10 million. (*paragraph 3*)

f) I hope you haven't changed your m_____ about helping me. (*paragraph 3*)

g) She inherited an absolute f_____ from her grandmother. (*paragraph 4*)

h) The teacher h_____ back the homework the next day. (*paragraph 5*)

The Conservative Party announced today that it had received £5 million from the millionaire John Paul Getty II. This is the first time that Getty has donated money to a political party. Getty, who is the son of an American oil billionaire, described his love for "the British way of life." In a statement, he said, "I hope that my donation will help to enable the new leader to deliver a Conservative victory in the next election." The Conservatives, after a disastrous last election and long arguments about a new leader, will be grateful for all the help they can get.

Getty is famous for giving away enormous amounts of money. A number of years ago, he gave £50 million to the National Gallery and £20 million to the British Film Institute. In addition, each year, he gives away more than £1 million to drug addicts, the homeless, and other people in need. "As long as I have money, I will give it away," he once said.

His private life has been full of drama. He has been married three times—his second wife died of drugs. His son was kidnapped by the Mafia, and the grandfather refused to pay. Getty Senior changed his mind when one of the boy's ears was cut off and sent to a newspaper.

After years of wild living, Getty discovered God and converted to Catholicism. At the same time, he learned that a reorganization of the family fortune had left him with £300 million. He created a charity to manage the distribution of his money.

In 1998, he handed back his American passport and became a British citizen. He admits that the Britain he loves (the Britain of cricket and warm beer) is not the Britain that exists today. Will the Conservative Party be able to return Britain to the romantic past? They will need to win an election first.

Vocabulary

1 Circle the best alternative.

Example
We don't take credit cards; we only take
money /(cash)/ fortune.

a) He *inherited / interested / invested* some money
   from his grandmother and bought a new
   house with it.
b) I must remember to pay the electricity
   account / bill / tax this week!
c) The *pension / profit / rent* for an apartment in
   the middle of Manhattan is extremely high.
d) They made a big *cash / profit / salary* from the
   sale of their house.
e) We want to buy a new car, so we try to
   inherit / lend / save some money every month.
f) What's the *currency / exchange rate / worth* for
   the dollar?
g) When she retired, her *pension / salary / value*
   wasn't enough to live on.
h) Why don't you *earn / grow / invest* some of
   your money instead of spending it all?
i) She doesn't *make / win / manage* much money,
   but she likes the job.

2 Complete the story with words from the box.

band	single	canceled	charts	concert
fans	gigs	lead	album	tour

In 1976, the punk (a) _____ the Sex Pistols
recorded their first (b) _____ , *Anarchy in
the UK*. Although they had a few
(c) _____ , the Sex Pistols were not
famous until they appeared on TV in December
of that year. The record company EMI
(d) _____ the group's contract because of
the disgusting things they said on the TV
program. With a new record company, their next
record, *God Save the Queen*, went to the top of the
(e) _____ , but it was banned by the BBC
because it criticized the Queen. On the day of the
Queen's silver anniversary, the group organized a
(f) _____ on a boat on the River Thames,
but they were arrested by the police. After three
more hits, they released all their songs on an
(g) _____ , which was also very
successful. There were more problems with the
police, and many towns banned
(h) _____ by the group. After a short
(i) _____ of the U.S., the (j) _____
singer, Johnny Rotten, decided to leave.

3 Match the sentence beginnings in box A with
their endings in box B.

A

a)	At the end of the concert, they gave
b)	He wants to give
c)	It's very difficult to come
d)	She has always wanted to go
e)	The concert was sold
f)	The group decided to split
g)	The group's new record is coming
h)	They only had one hit, but they kept

B

1	out next week.
2	on making records for fifteen years.
3	away free T-shirts.
4	out two weeks ago.
5	out with a rock star.
6	up after two years together.
7	up his job in the bank and join a band.
8	up with an original idea for a music video.

4 Complete each sentence by making a noun from
the word in parentheses.

Example
The thieves stole his <u>collection</u> (collect) of antique
furniture.

a) Matt announced his _____ (decide)
   to pursue a solo career.
b) Our last vacation was a complete
   _____ (disastrous).
c) Many mothers look for part-time
   _____ (employ) when their children
   are young.
d) Mandela finally won his _____ (free)
   after twenty-six years in prison.
e) The singer was given a bouquet of roses at
   the end of the _____ (perform).
f) It is hard to explain the _____
   (popular) of some pop bands.
g) They are going to buy a house near the ocean
   for their _____ (retire).
h) The band bought a new van to transport all
   their _____ (equip).

Writing

1 Where do the phrases below belong in the letter? Write the number in the box.

a) Could you please tell me ☐

b) Finally, I would appreciate it if you could send me ☐

c) First of all, I would like to know a little more about ☐

d) For instance, ☐

e) I am writing in reference to ☐ 1

f) I look forward to hearing from you soon. ☐

g) I would be grateful if you would send me ☐

h) In addition, I would appreciate more information about ☐

Dear Sir/Madam,

....(1).... your advertisement in the newspaper yesterday. I am interested in applying for a grant, and ....(2).... some information.

....(3).... the Fund. Your advertisement says that it is for young people. ....(4).... how old I must be to apply? I am going to be 18 next month. ....(5).... the kinds of projects that you support. ....(6).... , is it possible to receive a grant to help with my college education?

....(7).... an application form.

....(8).... .

Sincerely,

Cosmo Brickett

Cosmo Brickett

---

2 Look at the advertisement and notes and write a letter asking for more information.

What kind of work?   Travel – who pays?

VOLUNTARY
Work Camps

Learn new skills and a new language at our international voluntary work camps

Our volunteer work program offers a huge range of possibilities to responsible young people who want to discover the world and make it a better place to live.

Your housing will be in our dormitories, and all meals are provided.

Programs start in July, September, and January.

Don't delay – apply today!

Write to:

How long are the work camps?

Pronunciation

1 Read these song titles aloud, changing *going to* to *gonna*.

a) Who's Going to Stop the Rain? (Anastacia)

b) Your Time is Going to Come (Led Zeppelin)

c) I'm Going to Be Alright (Jennifer Lopez)

d) It's Going to Be Me ('N Sync)

🔊 Repeat the song titles after the recording.

2 🔊 Now listen to these song titles. What is *wanna* short for?

I Wanna Be Your Man (The Beatles)
Scream If You Wanna Go Faster (Geri Halliwell)
I Wanna Dance With Somebody Who Loves Me (Whitney Houston)
Wanna Get Paid (LL Cool J)

9 Rules

Grammar

1 For each situation below, check (✓) the correct consequence.

Example
Annie's English teacher was sick.
a) Annie didn't have to go to school that morning. ✓
b) Annie couldn't go to school that morning.

1 *The next day was a holiday.*
   a) She didn't have to go to work.
   b) She couldn't go to work.

2 *She wanted to go out, but her telephone wasn't working.*
   a) She didn't have to call anyone.
   b) She couldn't call anyone.

3 *Her best friend was in Cancún on vacation.*
   a) She didn't have to go and see her.
   b) She couldn't go and see her.

4 *It was too late to go to the movies.*
   a) She didn't have to go and see a movie.
   b) She couldn't go and see a movie.

5 *She had a lot of food in the fridge.*
   a) She didn't have to buy any food.
   b) She couldn't buy any food.

6 *Her apartment was extremely clean and neat.*
   a) She didn't have to clean it.
   b) She couldn't clean it.

2 Rewrite the sentences so that they refer to past time.

Example
All men must do two years of military service.
All men had to do two years of military service.

a) People can choose between the army and the navy.

_____

_____

b) All new soldiers have to have a medical examination.

_____

_____

c) You can't join the army if you have a physical handicap.

_____

_____

d) You cannot have long hair in the army.

_____

_____

e) Women don't have to do military service.

_____

_____

f) Foreigners don't have to register for military service.

_____

_____

Are any of these past or present sentences true for your country?

3 For each sentence, finish the second sentence so that it means the same as the first.

Example
Smoking is not allowed in the museum.
You can't (or *cannot* or *must not*) *smoke in the museum.*

a) We spent two hours waiting in line.
We had _____

_____ .

b) It's a good idea to arrive at the museum early in the morning.
You _____

_____ .

c) It wasn't necessary to get a guide.
We didn't _____

_____ .

d) I don't think it's a good idea to go there with young children.
You _____

_____ .

e) You can visit the museum without paying on Wednesdays.
On Wednesdays, you don't _____

_____ .

f) They didn't let us take any photos.
We _____

_____ .

Listening

1 [cassette] Cover the tapescript opposite and listen to a conversation between two men. Are the following sentences true or false?

a) Patrick went to a football game last night.

b) Patrick often talks to his wife about football.

c) Patrick doesn't know how to make his wife happy.

d) Brian thinks he understands women.

e) Brian has a good relationship with his wife.

2 [cassette] Brian gives Patrick advice about women. Listen again and check (✓) the pieces of advice that you hear.

Examples
Talk to your wife about football.
Work fifteen hours a day.

a) Don't give your wife any money.

b) Never do any housework.

c) Don't forget your wife's birthday.

d) Buy flowers for your wife.

e) Tell your wife that her hair looks nice.

f) Tell your wife to go on a diet.

g) Be nice to your wife's friends.

h) Don't complain about the telephone bills.

Brian Where were you last night, Patrick? You missed a really great game.

Patrick Oh, I had to baby-sit.

Brian Baby-sit?

Patrick Yeah, Julie went out with her friends.

Brian Did you tell her it was an important game?

Patrick No, of course not. You can't talk to women about football—they just don't understand things like that.

Brian No, no, you're right, Pat.

Patrick You know, I don't think I understand women at all. Julie always seems to be fed up with me—I just don't know what I should do to make her happy.

Brian Oh, that's easy. You just have to work fifteen hours a day and give her all your money.

Patrick I do that anyway. And it's still not enough. Things were much easier for our dads. They didn't have to do any housework or cooking or shopping. I mean, I do loads of housework and she still isn't happy.

Brian Oh no, you can't do that! Women love complaining, and you have to give her something to complain about. I never do any housework.

Patrick Hey, Brian, what about equality and all that?

Brian Look, you don't have to do the housework to keep a woman happy. You just have to follow a few simple rules.

Patrick And what are these simple rules?

Brian Well, first of all, you cannot forget her birthday or your wedding anniversary. Buy flowers and take her out for a nice dinner.

Patrick O.K. Anything else?

Brian You have to notice her hair—tell her it looks nice. Oh, and ask her if she's lost weight. They love that.

Patrick Ha ha—yes, Julie's always on a diet.

Brian Wait a minute—that's not all. You have to be nice to her friends—but not too nice. And—this is a big one—you must not complain about the phone bills.

Patrick Ha ha. Very good! I suppose you have the perfect marriage!

Brian Uh, no, not really. Sharon left me three weeks ago.

Vocabulary

1 Match the adjectives in the box to the descriptions below.

cheerful	insecure	lazy	optimistic
sensible	sensitive	silly	~~talkative~~

Example
He never stops talking! *talkative*

a) She always thinks so carefully about everything she does!
b) She never wants to do any work!
c) He really understands other people and knows how to talk to them!
d) She thinks that everything will be fine!
e) He's always smiling and so happy!
f) She has no confidence in herself at all!
g) He's like a child—more like five years old than twenty-five!

2 Circle the best alternative.

Example
A lot of people borrow money to pay for their college *career /* education */ training*.

a) *Elementary / Education / High* schools are for children five to eleven years old.
b) Why do so many schoolchildren want to sit in the back of the *class / high school / program*?
c) *Colleges / Subjects / Lists* like music and art are always very popular.
d) Most students in the U.S. *fail / pass / take* exams called the SATs in high school.
e) In the United States, high school students are *fourteen to seventeen / eleven to thirteen / eighteen to twenty-one* years old.
f) At the end of each school year, students take a *final / mid-term / last* exam.
g) Many college *students / children / professors* live in dormitories on campus.

3 Complete each sentence with a preposition from the box.

about	for	for	in	of	on
~~to~~	to	with			

Example
According __to__ the rules in *How to Be the Perfect Ms. Right*, you must never ask a man out.

a) You shouldn't be too honest _____ your feelings.
b) I usually fall in love with men who are not good _____ me.
c) I disagree _____ the rules in the book.

d) Barbara had to say she was too busy to talk to Michael _____ the phone.
e) A boy from school invited me _____ his house.
f) Have you had enough _____ that cake or would you like some more?
g) Makiko's grandfather paid _____ her training.
h) They play an important role _____ preserving Japanese culture.

4 Match the book titles in box A to the subjects in box B. You will need to insert the missing vowels in box B.

A

a) *An Idiot's Guide to Einstein's Relativity*
b) *Banking and Finance Today*
c) *Great Rivers of the World*
d) *Pi—the Magic Number*
e) *The Molecular Structure of Carbon*
f) *The Sex Life of Giant Pandas*
g) *Was Napoleon Murdered?*

B

1 b _ _ l _ gy
2 ch _ m _ stry
3 _ c _ n _ m _ cs
4 g _ _ gr _ phy
5 h _ st _ ry
6 m _ th
7 phys _ cs

5 Complete each sentence with an appropriate form of the word in parentheses.

Example
Stop looking so <u>miserable</u> (misery)!

a) Follow my _____ (advise) and you won't have any problems.
b) The train arrives at _____ (exact) nine o'clock.
c) People in big cities are not always very _____ (friend).
d) Every summer during my _____ (child), we went on vacation to Atlantic City.
e) It was one of the most _____ (embarrass) experiences of my life.
f) Her parents didn't want her to marry a _____ (foreign).
g) She wore a _____ (tradition) white dress at her wedding.

Writing

1 Read the letter and replace each of the underlined phrases 1–10 with a phrase from the list below (a–j).

Dear Nicky,

(1) _Thanks so much for writing._ (2) _It was good to hear your news._ (3) _I'm sorry I haven't written in so long,_ but (4) _I've been really busy._

My big news is that I split up with Michael. At first, I was really sad, but I feel much better about it now. I met a really nice guy the other day, but I don't think I'm ready for another boyfriend right now. I have so much work to do that I don't have the time!

Well, (5) _that's all the news for now,_ but (6) _I promise I'll write again soon._ (7) _I have to stop now._ By the way, Doris (8) _sends her love._ (9) _Take care and write back soon._

(10) _All the best,_
Barbara

a) asked me to say hi ☐
b) Best wishes ☐
c) I have to go ☐
d) I'll be in touch soon ☐
e) I've had so much to do ☐
f) I was really happy to read your news ☐
g) Be well and keep in touch ☐
h) Many thanks for your letter ☐1
i) Sorry it's been so long since I last wrote ☐
j) that's about it ☐

2 In informal writing, it is usual to use contractions. Circle all the contractions in Barbara's letter. What are the uncontracted (full) forms?

contracted form	_full form_
I'm	I am
_____	_____
_____	_____
_____	_____
_____	_____

3 Imagine that you are Barbara's friend. Write a reply to her letter. In the second paragraph of your letter, tell her your own personal news.

Pronunciation

Underline all the negative verbs that you can contract in the song titles below.

Example
<u>Cannot</u> Be With You Tonight _(can't)_

a) I Could Not Live Without Your Love
b) It Does Not Have to Be This Way
c) Love Does Not Have to Hurt
d) She Does Not Have to Try
e) We Really Should Not Be Doing This
f) You Cannot Hurry Love
g) You Did Not Have to Be So Nice
h) You Did Not Have to Go
i) You Do Not Have to Say You Love Me
j) You Do Not Have to Worry

🔲 Repeat the song titles with the contracted verbs after the recording.

10 *Review 2*

Grammar

1 Look at the sign in each question and choose the best explanation.

❶

LEAVE KEYS AT THE FRONT DESK

a) You couldn't leave your keys at the front desk.
b) You don't have to take your keys out of the hotel.
c) You didn't have to leave your keys at the front desk.
d) You must not take your keys out of the hotel.

❷

Everything must go!

a) They have already sold everything.
b) They want to sell everything.
c) Everybody is going to leave.
d) They aren't going anywhere.

❸

CLOSED
VISIT US AT OUR NEW LOCATION AT
334 MAIN STREET

a) The store is moving to a new building soon.
b) The new store is going to close soon.
c) The store has moved to a new building recently.
d) The new store is not going to move to Main Street.

❹

MAXIMUM WEIGHT
200 POUNDS

a) Don't put things here that are heavier than 200 pounds.
b) Don't put things here if they don't weigh as much as 200 pounds.
c) The lightest weight that you can put here is 200 pounds.
d) Put things here if they are heavier than 200 pounds.

❺

BUY NOW, PAY LATER
0% INTEREST

a) You can pay the interest if you buy now.
b) You don't have to spend any money until later.
c) You can't pay any interest if you buy later.
d) You shouldn't buy anything now.

❻

Castle *Pizzeria*
BEST PRICES IN TOWN

a) Pizzas are not as cheap here as in other pizzerias.
b) Other pizzerias are not as expensive as here.
c) You can buy the most expensive pizzas here.
d) Pizzas are more expensive in other pizzerias.

2 Each sentence has one word that should not be there. Cross it out.

Example
Could you explain ~~me~~ how to send an e-mail?

a) Did you to have to wear a uniform in high school?
b) Have you been go to the movies recently?
c) I couldn't to invite my friends to my house.
d) I don't bother to going to supermarkets anymore.
e) I'm not definitely not going to forget my real friends.
f) Matt is having eat lunch with Madonna and Guy on Monday.
g) My husband bought to me a silver bracelet for my birthday.
h) She is not hardly ever at home in the evenings.
i) I was wrote an angry letter to the bank yesterday.
j) There shouldn't to be different rules for men and women.
k) We were studied this with our teacher last year.

3 Rewrite the sentences, beginning with the words given.

Example
We're not allowed to speak English in our German classes.
We must *not speak English in our German classes.*

a) Last week, my brother borrowed 20 dollars from me.
Last week, I _____

_____

b) Unfortunately, it wasn't possible for me to finish the exercise.
Unfortunately, I _____

_____

c) I learned Spanish from my mother.
My mother _____

_____

d) It wasn't necessary for us to take the car.
We did _____

_____

e) She rarely arrives on time.
She hardly _____

_____

f) What are your plans for the weekend?
What are you _____

_____

g) I bought a cheap watch from a man in the street.
A man in the street _____

_____

h) I think it's a good idea for you to call him.
I think you _____

_____

i) You can get into the museum without paying after five o'clock.
You don't _____

_____

4 Complete the story by filling in each blank with one word only.

We live in a very quiet village. We _hardly_ ever have any visitors, and many of the villagers have never been farther (a) _____ the nearest town. But the older villagers have (b) _____ forgotten about the day that Princess Caraboo came to town. My grandmother (c) _____ me the story.

When the Princess arrived in the village, nobody (d) _____ understand her, because she spoke a very strange language. But the villagers did (e) _____ have to wait long, because a few days later, a Portuguese sailor also arrived. "I (f) _____ been to her country," he said. "I will tell (g) _____ what she is saying. She comes from the island of Javasu, and pirates brought (h) _____ here. Now, she is hoping to stay here to find peace."

She made many friends, and the owner of the local castle said, "She is a princess, and we (i) _____ look after her. She can stay with me, and she will not have (j) _____ worry about money."

For a long time, everybody was happy. Then, one day, a journalist showed a newspaper story and a photo to the castle owner. The photo looked just (k) _____ Princess Caraboo.
"Yes," she admitted, "it is me. But believe me, I (l) _____ never done anything like this before. My father is a poor man from another town. He dressed me in these clothes, and he brought (m) _____ here to look for my fortune. My brother had to pretend to be a sailor."
"I will never (n) _____ anyone your secret," replied the castle owner. "And I love (o) _____ with a princess. Will you marry me?"

Suddenly I realized that my grandmother was talking about herself. My grandfather kept his word, and I am the only person that my grandmother has (p) _____ told.

Vocabulary

1 Choose the best alternative from the options below to fill in the blanks.

At the St. Louis Olympic Games of 1904, it was a hot, <u>humid</u> day, and there were thirty-two athletes in the (a) _____ . Most of the (b) _____ had to (c) _____ before the end, but fourteen of them made it to the finish. One of them was a New Yorker, Fred Lorz.

Fred started feeling ill during the race, but (d) _____ for him a car stopped and gave him a (e) _____ . As he walked into the (f) _____ , people thought he was the (g) _____ . His (h) _____ was taken with the daughter of the President, and they were going to give him the (i) _____ . But just then, someone (j) _____ that Fred hadn't bothered running the whole race—he had covered eleven miles as a passenger in a car. When the crowd (k) _____ that Fred had (l) _____ his victory in this (m) _____ way, they became (n) _____ and angry. Lorz had trouble leaving the stadium, and he was not (o) _____ to run again for a long time.

Example

(humid)   rather   warm

- a) athletics   human   marathon
- b) careers   divers   runners
- c) break down   come up   give up
- d) fortunately   recently   silly
- e) delivery   lift   speech
- f) neighborhood   stadium   studio
- g) challenge   winner   vet
- h) photograph   photographer   photography
- i) gold medal   running water   solo career
- j) found out   gave away   moved out
- k) disagreed   realized   suggested
- l) achieved   employed   respected
- m) dishonest   insecure   sensible
- n) decent   delighted   noisy
- o) awarded   allowed   applied

2 Complete the story with words from the box. You can use the words more than once.

about	at	for	in	into	of	on
over	to	up				

Two men were sitting in a bar talking _about_ their sons.

"My son was no good (a) _____ schoolwork at all," said the first man. "He was only interested (b) _____ music. He was crazy (c) _____ it. He joined a band, and his first song went straight (d) _____ the top (e) _____ the charts. He has plenty (f) _____ money now, and he doesn't know what to spend it (g) _____ . Just last week, he bought a new house (h) _____ his best friend!"

"Ah," said the second man. "I was worried (i) _____ my son, too. He dropped out (j) _____ school because he thought it was a waste (k) _____ time. But then he applied (l) _____ a job in a bank, and (m) _____ the years he's been really successful. (n) _____ fact, he's so rich now that he has just given his best friend a million dollars."

Just then, a third friend walked into the bar. "What does your son do (o) _____ a living?" they asked.

"My son? I'll tell you (p) _____ my son," said the third man. "He's a lazy good-for-nothing. He's had one or two jobs, but he always gets tired (q) _____ them after a week or two and gives them (r) _____ . But he has rich friends, and he always seems to have loads (s) _____ money. He's just moved (t) _____ a new house that one friend gave him, and another friend has just given him a million dollars!"

3 Complete each sentence by making an adjective from the word in parentheses.

Example
He's a <u>dangerous</u> (danger) driver who always breaks the speed limit.

a) He was much more _____ (confidence) after doing the training course.

b) Is it better to be rich or _____(fame)?

c) The waitress was very _____ (friend), and we left a good tip.

d) She tried to give up chocolate, but it only made her _____ (misery).

e) On a first date, you must be quiet and _____ (mystery).

f) Working in the maternity ward of a large hospital is a very _____ (stress) job.

g) The Beatles were one of the most _____ (success) bands of all time.

h) I was invited to a _____ (tradition) Japanese tea ceremony.

---

4 Complete the crossword. You have seen all the words that you need in Units 1–9 of *American Inside Out*. Some of the letters have been given to you.

Clues

Across
1 place for actors in a theater (5)
3 frozen water (3)
5 see picture 5 (6)
9 see picture 9 (4)
10 CD/record with lots of songs (5)
11 not dry (3)
12 to begin with (2,5)
14 angry/unhappy (5)
15 take part in an election (4)
18 makes a store ready for business in the morning (5,2)
20 connected with love (8)
22 the military (4)
23 behaved (5)
24 making money (7)
25 opposite of *near* (3)
26 not dead (5)
27 opposite of *fat* (4)
28 see picture 28 (6)
29 put numbers together (3)
30 spend (money or time) badly (5)

Down
1 see picture 1 (10)
2 pop concert (3)
4 from China (7)
6 country in north Africa (5)
7 see picture 7 (6)
8 very long race (8)
13 see picture 13 (4)
16 what a person looks like (10)
17 not agree (8)
19 identity (4)
21 with lines like a zebra (7)
22 suggestions/ recommendations (6)
24 the same (5)
27 a hot drink (3)

11 Smile

Grammar

1 Test your knowledge of social customs around the world. Add *always* or *never* to each sentence.

Examples
Stop at a red light. *Always stop at a red light.*
Drink and drive. *Never drink and drive.*

a) Call the waiter *garçon* in a French cafe.

b) Cross your knife and fork after a meal in Italy.

c) Eat with your left hand in north Africa.

d) Give a tip to New York taxi drivers.

e) Try to speak Spanish if you are a tourist in Mexico.

f) Be on time if you are invited to someone's home in the United States.

g) Take off your shoes when you go into a Japanese house.

h) Kiss your colleagues at business meetings in China.

2 Look at the example. Some phrasal verbs do not take a direct object. Cross out the words in *italics* that should not be there. Four sentences are correct.

Example
Can you hold on ~~the telephone~~ and I'll get a pen?

a) I ran after *the bus,* but unfortunately I missed it.

b) I think I'll stay up *the evening* and watch the late-night movie on TV.

c) I think it's better to deal with *the problem* now.

d) Turn off *the light* before you go out.

e) Why don't you sit down *the chair* and rest?

f) They decided to split up *their relationship* after three years together.

g) They called off *the wedding* because her father was sick.

3 Rewrite the phrases in *italics*, inserting the pronoun in parentheses in the correct place.

Example
A: Two strawberry ice cream cones, please.
B: Strawberry? I'm sorry, *we've completely run out of.* (it)
   <u>we've completely run out of it</u>

a) A: What size is this, please?
   B: It's a size 12. *Would you like to try on?* (it)
   _____

b) A: Is it serious?
   B: No, just stay in bed for a few days and *you'll soon get over.* (it)
   _____

c) A: We'll be happy to exchange your shirt if you show us the receipt.
   B: Oh, no. *I think I threw away!* (it)
   _____

d) A: You're just like your mother—*you really take after!* (her)
   B: And you're like your mother, too—bossy and selfish!
   _____

e) A: Is everything all right with your dinner, sir?
   B: Yes, fine, but the music is very loud— *could you turn down, please?* (it)
   _____

f) A: You're not going out in that old coat, are you?
   B: Why not? I like it. *I'm not going to take off* just because you don't like it. (it)
   _____

g) A: Yes, I smoke a little, but only about thirty a day.
   B: Thirty cigarettes a day! *You have to give up immediately!* (them)
   _____

Reading

1 Read the article about the Mona Lisa and match the paragraph titles to the paragraphs.

a) Is the Mona Lisa a Copy? (*paragraph* _3_)
b) Who Really Was the Mona Lisa? (*paragraph* ___)
c) The Birth of a Painting (*paragraph* ___)
d) The French Connection (*paragraph* ___)
e) The Secret of the Smile (*paragraph* ___)

2 Read the article again and decide if the following sentences are true (T) or false (F).

a) Leonardo painted the Mona Lisa about five hundred years ago. ☐

b) He painted it very quickly. ☐

c) The Mona Lisa is a portrait of Vasari's wife. ☐

d) Louis XIV put the painting in the palace at Fontainebleau. ☐

e) The Louvre has not always been a museum. ☐

f) The thief wrote a letter to an American gallery. ☐

g) The Mona Lisa is possibly a self-portrait of Leonardo. ☐

h) You can't see the Mona Lisa's mouth very well. ☐

3 Look at the pronouns in *italics* in the article. What do they refer to?

Example
her (line 6) *the Mona Lisa*

a) it (line 12) _____

b) him (line 14) _____

c) it (line 20) _____

d) it (line 22) _____

e) she (line 41) _____

f) they (line 46) _____

The Mona Lisa

The world's most famous smile—and the world's most famous painting—is Leonardo's Mona Lisa (La
5 *Gioconda). But how much do you know about **her**? Who is the mysterious woman, and why is her smile so special?*

10 **1** Leonardo began work on this portrait around 1500 and spent many years working on *it*. According to the art historian Vasari, it is the portrait of the young wife of a merchant from Florence, but Leonardo never gave **him**
15 the picture. He kept it for himself.

2 Later the French king bought it and put it in the royal palace at Fontainebleau. Centuries later, the French king Louis XIV moved the palace to Versailles, and the painting moved
20 too. For a while, Napoleon had *it* in his bedroom, but the Mona Lisa moved to the Louvre when *it* became a museum. It has not moved since then, apart from a few years at the beginning of the twentieth century.

25 **3** In 1911, the painting was stolen. It could not be found anywhere, but in 1913 the thief sent a letter to a gallery in Italy. He wanted to sell it. But why did the thief wait two years before returning it? During this time, many
30 copies of the painting were made and sold to American collectors. Is the painting now in the Louvre also a fake? Many people think that this is a real possibility.

4 Leonardo's painting is extremely life-like,
35 but many experts are not sure that it is a portrait of the woman from Florence. There are many theories, but perhaps the most interesting is that it is a portrait of Leonardo himself. An American expert has compared
40 Leonardo's self-portrait and the Mona Lisa, and **she** has found that many of the features are exactly the same.

5 The two most important features of a face are the corners of the eyes and the mouth. If
45 you look at the painting, you will see that these features are blurred—**they** are much less clear than the rest of the face. As a result, the viewer has to imagine what the Mona Lisa is thinking. The mystery of her smile is just a
50 bit of clever artistic technique.

Vocabulary

1 Put the following parts of the face in order. Begin with the top of the face and end with the facial feature at the bottom of the face.

> cheek   ~~chin~~   eyebrow   eyelash
> ~~forehead~~   lip   mustache   teeth

      <u> forehead </u>   d) <u>   </u>

a) <u>   </u>   e) <u>   </u>

b) <u>   </u>   f) <u>   </u>

c) <u>   </u>   <u> chin </u>

2 Read the character description for your astrological sign. Do you agree with it?

NUMEROLOGICAL
Astrology

Add the four numbers of the year of your birth together, e.g., 1972 1+9+7+2 = 19. Find the Numerological Astrological sign that corresponds to you.

Earth 0–15

You are a hard-working, sensible realist. You are a loyal friend, but you are also ambitious at work. You are a little shy, but you enjoy being with other people, who like your sense of humor.

Air 16–20

You are an easygoing kind of person—sociable and a lot of fun to be with. You like to laugh, and you are confident in most social situations. You are not always very sensitive, and some people may think you are selfish.

Fire 21–24

You have a very warm personality, sometimes too warm, and some of your relationships are very stormy. At times, you are miserable and look for arguments with your friends or partner. You don't like bossy people, and you don't like being in crowds.

Water 25–30

You are a secretive person, and you may appear mysterious to people who do not know you well. You do not have enemies, and you have a natural authority, but you find it hard to talk about yourself. You appear strong, although you are not always very sure of yourself.

---

3 Look in the text in exercise 2 to find adjectives for the following nouns.

noun	adjective
ambition	<u>ambitious</u>
a) confidence	<u> </u>
b) loyalty	<u> </u>
c) misery	<u> </u>
d) mystery	<u> </u>
e) secret	<u> </u>
f) strength	<u> </u>
g) warmth	<u> </u>

4 Cross out the noun phrases on the right that **cannot** be used with the phrasal verbs on the left.

Example
call off   *a meeting / a party / ~~a problem~~*

a) fill out   *an application / a form / a mess*

b) get over   *an illness / a problem / money*

c) give up   *music lessons / smoking / a coat*

d) put on   *a form / some music / your shoes*

e) turn on   *a computer / smoking / the TV*

f) take off   *your clothes / a test / your watch*

g) turn up   *a job / the music / the volume*

5 Complete each sentence with a particle from the box.

> after   away   away   down   off   ~~up~~
> up   with

Example
Don't leave your coat on the floor—hang it <u>up</u> .

a) Just sit _____ and relax—everything will be all right in a minute.

b) The teacher told the students to put their books _____ and get ready for the test.

c) She takes _____ her mother—their personalities are the same.

d) They turned _____ the TV and finally went to bed.

e) This room is a real mess—clean it _____ immediately!

f) We really don't have time to deal _____ that problem right now.

g) Why don't you throw _____ those old shoes and get some new ones?

Writing

1 Look at the three invitations below. For each invitation, underline the information you need to answer these questions.

- Who is the invitation from?
- What is the invitation for?
- When is the event?

Colonel and Mrs. R. Peacock

Request the pleasure of the company of

Roger & Tania Hunt

at the wedding of their daughter, Rosemary,
to Mr. Jeremy Strutt on April 1 at 11:00 A.M.
at the Community Church, 14 Ridge Road, Dallas
RSVP

WILD GANGSTERS' PARTY
JOIN DAVID AND JEFF TO RING
IN THE NEW YEAR

DECEMBER 31 (FROM 9 P.M.)
BRING A BOTTLE (OR TWO)

P.S. WE HAVE PLENTY OF SPARE
ROOMS IF YOU NEED TO STAY
OVERNIGHT. PLEASE LET US KNOW
IF YOU'RE PLANNING TO COME.
THE OLD BARN, 45 TREETOP LANE,
NEW HOPE, PA

Brenda,
The office is holding the annual Christmas party on December 21 this year. They've hired the Ministry of Dance, and they have a really good DJ. It would be great if you could come. Ask Pedro to take care of the baby—he hates dancing anyway.

Let me know before the end of the week if you're coming.

Love,
Helen

P.S. Why don't you get your answering machine fixed?!

---

2 Look at two replies to the invitations. Some sentences are missing. Find the places (1–6) where the missing sentences (a–f) belong.

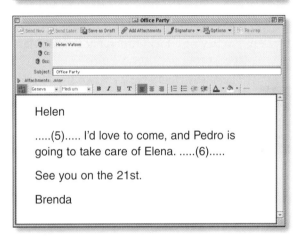

Dear Colonel and Mrs Peacock,

.....(1)..... Unfortunately, Roger and I will be in Mexico at the beginning of April, so I'm afraid we won't be able to make it. .....(2).....

Please give our best wishes to the happy couple. .....(3).....

.....(4).....

Tania Hunt

Helen

.....(5)..... I'd love to come, and Pedro is going to take care of Elena. .....(6).....

See you on the 21st.

Brenda

---

a) I hope that everything goes well.
b) I'm writing to thank you for the invitation to Rosemary's wedding.
c) Thanks for the e-mail.
d) We'll be in touch when we get back.
e) I'm really looking forward to it.
f) Sincerely yours,

3 Now write a reply to David and Jeff's invitation.

Pronunciation

 Listen to the tongue twisters below and practice saying them.

What noise annoys an oyster most?
A noisy noise annoys an oyster most.
Busy buzzing bumblebees.

12 Rebel

Grammar

1 Four of the sentences below contain a grammatical mistake. Correct the sentences that are wrong.

Example

~~Are you having~~ Do you have Internet access in your home?
They were having a party when we arrived. ✓

a) He is having a poster of Anna Kournikova on his bedroom wall.

b) How many countries are having nuclear weapons?

c) I'm having a lot of fun in my English classes this year.

d) She always looks happy when she's having a good time.

e) She was having a boyfriend who worked in a circus last year.

f) She was having a relationship with an older man when I last saw her.

g) She was having some difficulties with the exercise until I helped her.

h) She is having pink hair and a ring in her nose.

2 Circle the correct verb form.

James Dean *made only* / *was made only* three movies in his short life, but he (a) *remains* / *is remained* a legend of the cinema. He (b) *knows best* / *is best known* for his role in *Rebel Without a Cause*, where he (c) *plays* / *is played* the part of a rebellious teenager.

Dean was born in 1931. His mother (d) *died* / *was died* when he was young, and he (e) *brought up* / *was brought up* by his aunt and uncle. After high school, he (f) *went* / *was gone* to California, where he (g) *accept* / *was accepted* at the Actors'

Studio, a famous acting school. After a few jobs in TV dramas, he (h) *saw* / *was seen* by Warner Brothers and (i) *gave* / *was given* his first movie role, in *East Of Eden*. He (j) *became* / *was become* a star almost immediately, but it was the beginning of a very short career. In 1955, at the age of 24, he (k) *killed* / *was killed* in a car crash.

3 Put the verbs in parentheses into the simple past tense. In each sentence, one verb is active and the other is passive.

Example
In 1955, Che Guevara <u>joined</u> (join) Fidel Castro's Cuban rebels in Mexico, and he <u>was trained</u> (train) as a soldier.

a) A year later, the rebels _____ (land) in Cuba, and Che _____ (name) commander of the army.

b) The following year, the Cuban dictator Batista _____ (defeat), and Castro _____ (become) president.

c) After the revolution, Che's first book _____ (publish), and he _____ (become) a minister in the government.

d) For a few years, he _____ (travel) to many different countries, where he _____ (welcome) by socialist heads of state.

e) In 1965, he _____ (join) a guerrilla army in the Congo, but the army _____ (defeat) by government soldiers.

f) Two years later in Bolivia, his guerrilla army _____ (win) two battles against the government, but his friend, Régis Debray, _____ (catch).

g) A month later, the guerrillas _____ (fight) the Bolivian army again, and Che _____ (kill).

h) The news _____ (announce) the next day, but many people _____ (not believe) it until much later.

Listening and reading

1 🔲 Cover the tapescript opposite and listen to a radio interview. Match it to one of the newspaper cuttings below.

Anti-Globalization Leader Arrested

The well-known Dutch activist Sandra Van Praag has been arrested following a violent demonstration outside a McDonald's in Strasbourg. Van Praag was held overnight and will appear in court later today. In a statement to the press, a lawyer for Ms. Van Praag said that she had been charged with violent

Peaceful Demonstration Turns Violent

It is believed that as many as 70 anti-globalization protesters have been arrested in Strasbourg following violent clashes with the police. The demonstration outside the European Parliament began peacefully, but fighting broke out when protesters set fire to a car in front of the parliament building. A police

2 🔲 Listen again and complete each sentence with a past participle.

Example
Nine police officers were _injured_.

a) Two million euros of damage was
   _____ to stores and cars.

b) Permission was not _____ for the march.

c) Many people were _____ in the French and American revolutions.

d) Cars were _____ on fire.

e) A McDonald's was _____ by French activists.

f) Four French activists were _____ to prison.

3 Put the following words and phrases in the appropriate places in the tapescript. The first one has been done for you.

a fairer system	a group	anti-police
a peaceful protest	our cause	the law
~~the organizers~~	demonstrators	leaflets

Host Our guest today is Sandra Van Praag, one of _the organizers_ of the demonstration that took place in Strasbourg yesterday. Sandra—seventy-four
(a) _____ were arrested, nine police officers were injured, and over two million euros of damage was done to stores and cars. Is the violence necessary?

Sandra I think that the violence is unfortunate. The demonstration began as
(b) _____ march. We were handing out (c) _____ outside the European Parliament, and the police wanted to stop us. There was a happy, party atmosphere until the police began arresting people.

Host But permission was not given for the march. The government said no. The police were just doing their job, weren't they?

Sandra We're not (d) _____ , but sometimes it is necessary to break the law if you really care about your cause. Look at the French Revolution, look at the American Revolution. Think about Nelson Mandela. There was fighting, there was violence, many people were killed, but afterward, there was
(e) _____ .

Host In other words, you encourage people to break (f) _____ ?

Sandra It is true that cars were set on fire, but I do not support the people who did this. I am against the people who throw stones at the police. Much of this violence is just stupid, young people having what they call fun. But sometimes, yes. A few years ago, a McDonald's was attacked by
(g) _____ of French activists. They took it to pieces. Four of them were sent to prison, but their action was important—and successful. Since that time, people have started talking a lot more about…

Host And was your march yesterday successful?

Sandra I think that 30,000 people is a success, yes. (h) _____ has received a lot of publicity and…

Host Sandra, I'm afraid we've run out of time there. Thank you for joining us on the program. And now…

Vocabulary

1 Complete the text with words from the box.

about	against	at	away	in	into
~~of~~	of	out	to	with	

I became a member _of_ ATTAC because I care
(a) _____ the situation in some countries that
have gotten (b) _____ serious debt. I'm (c) _____
the globalization of the world economy, and I
decided to take part (d) _____ the
demonstration. The members of ATTAC are
supporters (e) _____ peaceful action, and we
disagree (f) _____ violence. Unfortunately, some
demonstrators broke (g) _____ from the march,
and violence broke (h) _____ . They started
throwing stones (i) _____ the police, and they
even set fire (j) _____ a car in the street.

2 Combine a word from box A with a word from
box B to make a compound noun. Then use the
compound nouns to complete the sentences
below.

A

| ~~animal~~ |
| recycling |
| police |
| fur |
| nuclear |
| plastic |
| protest |
| public |
| high |

B

| bags |
| center |
| coats |
| unemployment |
| marches |
| officers |
| ~~testing~~ |
| transportation |
| weapons |

Example
Some companies have stopped _animal testing_ in
the development of beauty products.

a) _____ try to keep the
peace at public demonstrations.

b) On May Day in many countries, workers
demonstrate against low wages and
_____ .

c) Many people have stopped wearing
_____ because they are
against cruelty to animals.

d) In many cities in the U.S., trucks pick up
your paper and bottles and take them to a
_____ .

e) Spending more money on _____
_____ is a good way to reduce traffic
pollution.

f) Supermarkets give away millions of
_____ every day.

g) The last time that _____
were used was in 1945.

h) There have been _____
in Genoa, Porto Alegre, and Washington, D.C.
against globalization.

3 Complete each sentence with the noun form of
the word in parentheses.

Example
Everyone should have the right to a basic
education (educate).

a) Friends of the Earth is an _____
(organize) that cares about the environment.

b) Her _____ (fascinate) with the circus
started at an early age.

c) In some countries, there is no _____
(separate) of religion and politics.

d) Many British politicians support the
_____ (legalize) of cannabis.

e) The government announced their
_____ (decide) to ban smoking in
public places.

f) There is an _____ (exhibit) of Russian
revolutionary posters at the art gallery.

g) There was a _____ (reduce) in
financial aid to college students last year.

h) They put up the Christmas _____
(decorate) on December 1.

4 Put the sentences in the correct order to complete
the story.

a) He was held prisoner for thirty days.
b) He was released.
c) His family paid the ransom.
d) The judge sent them to prison.
e) The kidnappers were pardoned by the
president.
f) The police arrested the kidnappers.
g) The son of a businessman was kidnapped,
and his bodyguard was killed.
h) They were charged with kidnapping and
murder.

1	2	3	4	5	6	7	8
g							e

Writing

1 Look at the results of a survey that was conducted with a group of a hundred young adults. They were asked what they thought about the problems that they face today.

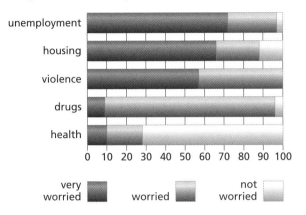

Complete the report, using words or phrases from the box.

> a few   ~~everybody~~   large number
> majority   most   nobody   none
> several   small number

A survey was conducted to find out what young people are most worried about.

The results of the survey show that nearly _everybody_ thought that unemployment was the biggest problem facing them. Only a

(a) _____ of people were not worried about it at all.

(b) _____ people thought that housing was also a big problem, but

(c) _____ said they didn't worry about it.

A (d) _____ of people were worried about violence, and

(e) _____ of the people interviewed said that it did not matter at all.

Only (f) _____ people were very worried about drugs, but almost

(g) _____ said this did not concern them at all. A few were also very worried about health, but the

(h) _____ were not concerned.

Maybe the most important information from the survey is that a lot of young people today are worried about a lot of things.

2 The survey also asked people about what was important in their lives. Look at the chart and write a short report about this information. Use as many words and phrases from the box in exercise 1 as possible.

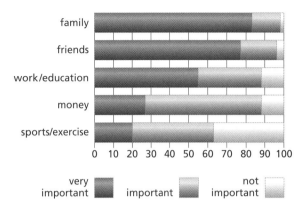

Pronunciation

Mark the main stress in the words in *italics*.

> Everybody's talking about
> *Missions, ambitions, traditions,* and *permissions,*
> Work *conditions, competitions.*
> All we are saying is…
>
> Everybody's talking about
> *Associations, corporations, obligations,*
> *Demonstrations, applications, populations,*
>   *destinations.*
> All we are saying is…

Listen to the recording to check your answers.

13 *Dance*

Grammar

1 Complete each sentence with *for* or *since*.

Example
I've had a headache <u>since</u> I woke up.

a) I haven't been to a beach _____ last summer.

b) I've been watching the football game _____ two hours.

c) I've had this book _____ a couple of months.

d) I haven't had a cup of coffee _____ early this morning.

e) I've known my best friend _____ we were very young.

f) I've lived in this town _____ three years.

g) I haven't seen my neighbor _____ the beginning of last week.

h) I've been studying English _____ about a year and a half.

Now rewrite the sentences so that they are true for you.

2 Fill in each blank with the correct past participle of the verb in parentheses.

a) Have you _____ (buy) your sister's birthday present yet?

b) He's never _____ (be) to a dance club.

c) I haven't _____ (go) to a rock concert in years.

d) I've never _____ (sing) on Broadway, but I've _____ (see) several plays on Broadway!

e) She's never _____ (meet) him, but they've talked on the phone several times.

f) That's the worst food we've ever _____ (eat)!

3 Complete the second sentence so that it means the same as the first. Use an appropriate form of the verb in parentheses.

Example
She started as a DJ two years ago.
She <u>has been a DJ for</u> two years. (be)

a) She became a fashion model in 1999.
She _____ 1999. (be)

b) She started being famous when she appeared on TV.
She _____ she appeared on TV. (be)

c) They got married forty-nine years ago.
They _____ forty-nine years. (be)

d) He arrived in New York on Friday.
He _____ Friday. (be)

e) I met him four years ago.
I _____ four years. (know)

f) When did he get the tattoo?
How long _____ the tattoo? (have)

4 Put each verb in parentheses into the present perfect or the present perfect continuous.

Example
She <u>has known</u> (know) him since they were in high school.

a) I _____ (be) a resident DJ for two years now.

b) I _____ (build) my own house, but it's not finished yet.

c) I _____ (save) money for my vacation, and I only need another $100.

d) I'm beat! I _____ (dance) all night.

e) Ibiza _____ (be) the clubbing capital of the world since the 1960s.

f) The club _____ (have) a roof for ten years.

Reading

1 Read the review of Billy Elliot and complete the cast list.

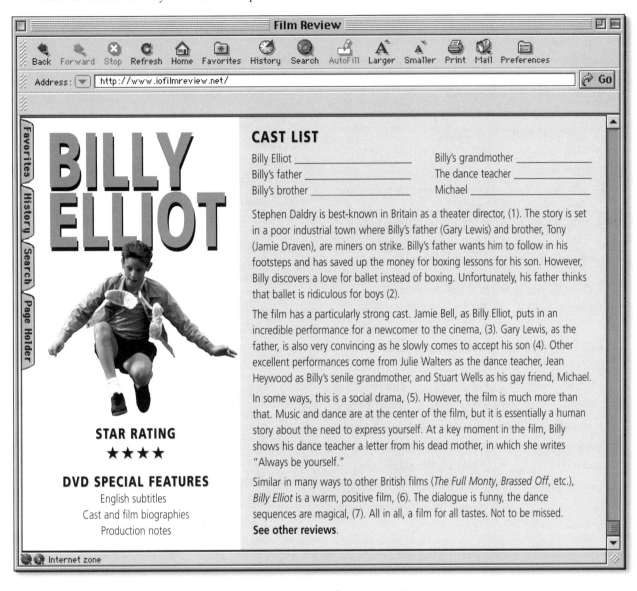

Film Review

Back Forward Stop Refresh Home Favorites History Search AutoFill Larger Smaller Print Mail Preferences

Address: http://www.iofilmreview.net/   Go

Favorites History Search Page Holder

BILLY ELLIOT

STAR RATING
★★★★

DVD SPECIAL FEATURES
English subtitles
Cast and film biographies
Production notes

CAST LIST

Billy Elliot _____   Billy's grandmother _____
Billy's father _____   The dance teacher _____
Billy's brother _____   Michael _____

Stephen Daldry is best-known in Britain as a theater director, (1). The story is set in a poor industrial town where Billy's father (Gary Lewis) and brother, Tony (Jamie Draven), are miners on strike. Billy's father wants him to follow in his footsteps and has saved up the money for boxing lessons for his son. However, Billy discovers a love for ballet instead of boxing. Unfortunately, his father thinks that ballet is ridiculous for boys (2).

The film has a particularly strong cast. Jamie Bell, as Billy Elliot, puts in an incredible performance for a newcomer to the cinema, (3). Gary Lewis, as the father, is also very convincing as he slowly comes to accept his son (4). Other excellent performances come from Julie Walters as the dance teacher, Jean Heywood as Billy's senile grandmother, and Stuart Wells as his gay friend, Michael.

In some ways, this is a social drama, (5). However, the film is much more than that. Music and dance are at the center of the film, but it is essentially a human story about the need to express yourself. At a key moment in the film, Billy shows his dance teacher a letter from his dead mother, in which she writes "Always be yourself."

Similar in many ways to other British films (*The Full Monty*, *Brassed Off*, etc.), *Billy Elliot* is a warm, positive film, (6). The dialogue is funny, the dance sequences are magical, (7). All in all, a film for all tastes. Not to be missed.
See other reviews.

Internet zone

2 Find the places (1–7) in the review where the following phrases could be added.

a) and the whole experience is a celebration of humanity ☐

b) and this is his first full-length work for the cinema 1

c) and his dancing is sensational ☐

d) and is less than pleased when he finds out about Billy's new interest ☐

e) and it leaves the audience feeling good as they come out of the cinema ☐

f) and we see the hardness of these working-class lives ☐

g) and finally helps him go to London for his dancing ☐

3 Check (✓) the topics below that are mentioned in the review.

a) similar films   f) the photography
b) the acting   g) the dancing
c) the film studio   h) the price
d) the dialogue   i) the special effects
e) the director   j) the story

4 Find words or phrases in the review that mean the same as the following.

a) most famous (*paragraph 1*)

b) do the same as him (*paragraph 1*)

c) stupid (*paragraph 1*)

d) put your feelings into words or actions (*paragraph 3*)

e) an important time (*paragraph 3*)

f) that everybody will like (*paragraph 4*)

Vocabulary

1 Match the words in the box to the descriptions below.

> flamenco   pop   reggae   rock 'n' roll
> samba   waltz

a) a Spanish dance to guitar music

b) a three-step dance for two people

c) carnival music from Brazil

d) music from the 1950s, made famous by Elvis Presley

e) the most famous performer of this Jamaican music was Bob Marley

f) the music of the Top Twenty and MTV

2 Complete the text with words from the box.

> clubs   dance floors   DJ   ~~famous~~
> House   live   nightlife   room   stage

London is <u>famous</u> for its (a) _____ , and one of the best-known (b) _____ is Bar Madrid. It has two (c) _____ and has (d) _____ for 575 people. Each night there is something different. On Mondays, for example, there is a choice between (e) _____ bands and a (f) _____ playing Brazilian music. On Tuesdays, which is student night, they play (g) _____ music, and on Thursdays, there are dancers on (h) _____ .

3 Complete each sentence with *at* or *on*.

Example
They first met <u>at</u> a friend's wedding.

a) He asked her to dance _____ the party after the wedding.

b) They spent the whole afternoon _____ the dance floor.

c) He spoke to her _____ the phone the next day.

d) She invited him to a ballet _____ the opera house.

e) Afterward, they had dinner _____ a restaurant near the opera.

f) The restaurant had a terrace _____ the roof.

g) They sat talking _____ the terrace until the restaurant closed.

h) The next evening, he took her to a club _____ a big hotel.

4 Replace the words in *italics* with an informal word or phrase from the box.

> guy   beat   laid-back   pretty   reckon
> broke   ~~winding him up~~

Example
She enjoyed *making him mad.*
She enjoyed winding him up.

a) His stamp collection is *very* good.

_____

_____

b) I met a really nice *man* on vacation last summer.

_____

_____

c) I *think* she used to be a hippie.

_____

_____

d) I was really *tired* after the party.

_____

_____

e) She was completely *out of money*, so she couldn't come on vacation with us.

_____

_____

f) She has a *very relaxed* approach to life.

_____

_____

5 Complete each sentence with a preposition from the box.

> about   ~~at~~   for   for   of   on   toward
> with

Example
Frank is very good <u>at</u> samba dancing.

a) How worried are you _____ your image?

b) How would you describe your attitude _____ dancing?

c) Miami is famous _____ its night clubs.

d) The club has room _____ 5,000 people.

e) The movie is based _____ a book by Stephen King.

f) The swimming pool is the size _____ a soccer field.

g) There's nothing wrong _____ ballet.

Writing

1   Look at the paragraph plan of a description of
    La Scala and put the paragraphs in the correct
    order.

    1   Introduction and location: *paragraph* ___
    2   General description: *paragraph* ___
    3   Things to see and do: *paragraph* ___

MILAN'S FAMOUS
La Scala

a

It was built in the eighteenth century and
has a beautiful facade. When you arrive,
you go into a beautiful foyer with palm
trees and huge mirrors. The interior of the
theater is decorated in red and gold and
has room for over 200 people.

b

Apart from the operas, you can also see
ballet and concerts of classical music.
There is an interesting theater museum,
and you can have guided tours of the
theater itself.

c

La Scala in Milan is one of the world's most
famous opera houses. It is situated in the
center of the city, not far from the
Cathedral.

2   Complete each sentence below with *because* or
    because of.

    Examples
    You need to reserve tickets in advance *because* it
    is so popular.
    La Scala closed for three years in 2002 *because of*
    construction work.

    a) It was called La Scala _____ a church
        that used to be on the site.
    b) The theater was rebuilt in 1945 _____ it
        had been damaged during the Second World
        War.
    c) Opera fans want to go there _____ it is
        the world's most famous theater.
    d) You can no longer stand at La Scala
        _____ fire regulations.
    e) December is a good time to visit _____
        there are many cultural events then.
    f) It's not a good idea to drive there _____
        the traffic problems in the center of Milan.

3   Write a short description (approximately
    a hundred words) of an interesting building in
    your town or a building that you know. Use the
    article about La Scala and the paragraph plan to
    help you.

Pronunciation

1   ▭ Listen to the short pronunciation of *for* in
    the phrases below.

    for ages   for two years   for a few days

    What is the short pronunciation of the underlined
    words in the phrases below?

    good at it   a lot of room   talk to me

    Listen to the recording to check.

2   ▭ Listen and repeat the sentences below,
    paying attention to the short pronunciation of the
    underlined words.

    a) What's your favorite place <u>for</u> dancing?
    b) Is your town famous <u>for</u> its nightlife?
    c) Do you prefer dancing <u>at</u> a club or a party?
    d) He pointed <u>at</u> a chair.
    e) What kinds <u>of</u> music do they play?
    f) It has a population <u>of</u> 80,000.
    g) I don't go <u>to</u> pop concerts.
    h) I haven't been <u>to</u> the beach yet.

14 *Call*

Grammar

1 For each situation below, choose the best question.

1 A man has put his bag on the seat of a bus. You want him to move it so that you can sit down. You say:

  a) Could you move your bag, please?
  b) Can I move your bag, please?
  c) Would you like me to move your bag, please?

2 You see a woman on the street outside your house. She looks lost. You say:

  a) Could you show me the way?
  b) Would you mind showing me the way?
  c) Would you like me to show you the way?

3 You are on top of the Empire State Building. You would like someone to take your picture. You say:
  a) Is it O.K. if I take your picture?
  b) Should I take your picture?
  c) Would you mind taking my picture, please?

4 A friend of yours says that she is feeling very sick. You say:

  a) I was wondering if you could call the doctor.
  b) Should I call the doctor?
  c) Would you mind calling the doctor?

5 Your car has broken down. You stop a person in the street. You say:

  a) Could you possibly help me push the car?
  b) Is it O.K. if I push your car?
  c) Would you like me to push your car?

2 Rewrite the questions, beginning with the words given.

Example
Does he love me?
Do you think <u>he loves me</u> ?

a) Will he return my call?

  Do you think _____

  _____ ?

b) What time is the meeting?

  Can you remember _____

  _____ ?

c) How much does a beer cost?

  Could you tell me _____

  _____ ?

d) Did he give her the message?

  Do you know _____

  _____ ?

e) What does "worried sick" mean?

  Do you know _____

  _____ ?

f) What do you think of my outfit?

  Could you tell me _____

  _____ ?

g) Who did you speak to?

  Can you remember _____

  _____ ?

3 Rearrange the words to make indirect questions.

Example
a any have idea is what Do
you Zoomatron ?
Do you have any idea what a Zoomatron is?

a) keys my I put Can remember car where you ?

  Can _____

  _____ ?

b) costs Do dollars how in know much this you ?

  Do _____

  _____ ?

c) Could is me tell the theater where you ?

  Could _____

  _____ ?

d) against Do is it law the think you ?

  Do _____

  _____ ?

e) Do if is know married she you ?

  Do _____

  _____ ?

Listening

1 📼 Cover the tapescript opposite and listen to three telephone conversations. Match the conversations to the "phone moans" below.

a) "I like to talk to a real person on the phone, but nowadays you get a recorded message which gives you all these options to choose from."

b) "I hate it when the person I'm speaking to starts drinking or eating something. It sounds disgusting!"

c) "I hate it when you call a company or an office and you can never get through to the person you want to speak to."

2 📼 Listen to the conversations again. When you hear a phrase, write the number of the conversation next to it.

a) Is…there, please? ☐1

b) Who's calling? ☐

c) I'd like to speak to… ☐

d) Could I speak to…? ☐

e) Sorry, she's not in right now. ☐

f) Thank you for calling. ☐

g) I'll connect you. ☐

h) Can you tell her I called, please? ☐

i) Please hold. ☐

j) You have the wrong extension. ☐

k) Can I take a message? ☐

l) No one is available to take your call… ☐

3 Write two short telephone conversations, using some of the phrases in exercise 2.

Conversation 1
A: Hello.
B: Oh, hello. Is Susan there, please?
A: Uh, just a moment. Who's calling?
B: It's Francesca. Is Susan in?
A: Uh, sorry, she's not in right now.
B: Oh, O.K. Can you tell her I called, please?
A: Yeah, sure. Can I take a message?
B: No, no thanks. Just "Francesca called," O.K.?
A: O.K. What did you say your name was?
B: Francesca. F-R-A-N-C-E-S-C-A.
A: O.K., I'll tell her. Bye.

Conversation 2
C: Oh, hello. I'd like to speak to someone…
D: This is Goldcard Financial services. Thank you for calling. If you have a touch-tone phone, please press the star key. If not, please hold…
Thank you. To report a stolen card, please press one. For billing, please press two. For all other services, please hold.
C: Oh, never mind.

Conversation 3
E: Good morning, XLCom. Can I help you?
F: Yes, good morning. Could I speak to someone in the technical support department, please?
E: Yes, of course. I'll connect you.
F: Thank you.
G: Hello. This is Dave.
F: Oh, hello. Is this the technical support department?
G: No. You have the wrong extension. Hang on and I'll connect you.
H: Hello.
F: Oh, hello. Is this the technical support department?
H: Yes.
F: Could I speak to the manager, please?
H: Speaking.
F: Ah, well, I have a problem with a new cell phone—
H: Ah, you need another department. This is the business network division. Hold on, please, and I'll connect you.
I: I'm afraid no one is available to take your call right now. Please leave your name and telephone number after the beep and we'll…

Vocabulary

1 Complete the text with words from the box.

> call   dialed   ~~directory~~   extension
> connection   message   cell phone
> operator   voice mail

I didn't have his number, so I called _directory_
assistance. The (a) _____ gave me his office
number. I (b) _____ the number, but his
(c) _____ was busy, and I had to leave a
(d) _____ on his (e) _____ . I asked
him to return my (f) _____ . Then I decided
to try his (g) _____ . I got through, but there
was a bad (h) _____ . When we finally
spoke, I couldn't remember why I wanted to talk
to him!

2 Complete each sentence with *said*, *told*, or *asked*.

Example
I _asked_ my parents for a cell phone for Christmas.

a) They _____ me that I was too young for a
phone.

b) I _____ that I needed one.

c) They _____ it was too expensive.

d) I _____ for a pay-as-you-go phone.

e) I _____ them that it was very cheap.

f) My father _____ no.

g) My mother _____ me if I minded.

h) I _____ her it was O.K.

i) I _____ I would ask my grandparents.

3 Complete each sentence with *at*, *in*, or *on*.

Example
He's not _at_ his desk right now.

a) Is it O.K. if I put you _____ hold?

b) Guess who I saw _____ the airport when I
was waiting for a taxi.

c) The line's busy—he's probably _____ the
Internet.

d) I probably won't be _____ work tonight.

e) What's that strange noise _____ the
background?

f) Where _____ earth have you been?

g) Why can't they leave us _____ peace?

h) You can always call me _____ an emergency.

i) I'll meet you _____ the station, outside the
main entrance, O.K.?

j) You've been _____ the phone for hours.

4 Complete each sentence with a verb from the
box.

> come   get   give   hang   ~~take~~   call
> pick   connect   run

Example
Yes, you can borrow my phone, but you have to
take care of it.

a) Can you _____ on and I'll see if he's
here?

b) Give me a call when you arrive and I'll come
and _____ you up.

c) I asked the operator to _____ me, but I
got cut off.

d) I'm going to keep leaving messages till he
calls me back—I refuse to _____ up.

e) I want to get one of those new miniature
phones that have just _____ out.

f) Send me an e-mail if you can't _____
me on the phone.

g) This is going to be quick—I've almost
_____ out of credit on my phone card.

h) Should I tell him to _____ you before
he leaves the office?

5 Put the conversation in the correct order.

a) Uhm…Could you take my number and ask
someone to call me back?

b) Good afternoon. Sharecare Babysitting
Services. Can I help you?

c) I'm afraid all the booking agents are busy
right now. Would you mind holding?

d) Thank you. Bye.

e) No problem, Mrs. Blair. I'll give the message
to one of the agents.

f) Certainly, ma'am. Could I have your name?

g) Yes, good afternoon. I'd like to have a
baby-sitter for this evening, please.

h) Yes, it's B-L-A-I-R, Blair. And the number is
(555) 055-4431.

1	2	3	4	5	6	7	8
b							d

Writing

1 [cassette icon] Cover the tapescript and listen to telephone conversations 1–3. Complete the messages below.

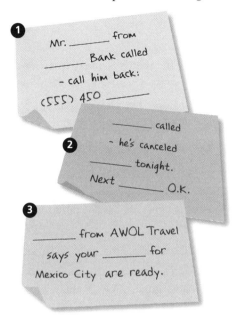

❶ Mr. _____ from _____ Bank called
– call him back:
(555) 450 _____

❷ _____ called
– he's canceled _____ tonight.
Next _____ O.K.

❸ _____ from AWOL Travel says your _____ for Mexico City are ready.

2 [cassette icon] Now listen to conversations 4 and 5 and take messages for each one.

Conversation 1
A: Hello.
B: Good afternoon. Could I speak to Mrs. Walton, please?
A: I'm afraid she's not in. Can I help?
B: Uh, I'm calling from Credit Bank. Could you tell me when she'll be back?
A: I'm not sure. Can I ask her to call you back?
B: That would be kind of you. My name's Lopez—that's L-O-P-E-Z—from Credit Bank, and the number is (555) 450-1010.
A: O.K., Mr. Lopez. I'll ask her to call you.
B: Thank you very much.
A: You're welcome. Bye.

Conversation 2
A: Hello.
C: Oh, hi. Is this Dave? It's Richard.
A: Hi, Richard. How are you?
C: Fine. And you?
A: Fine.
C: Is Karen in?
A: No, she went out somewhere. I think she'll be back about six. Do you want me to take a message?
C: Yeah, I have a lot of work at the office. Could you tell her that I can't play tennis tonight? I've already called the tennis club to cancel. Tell her I'm sorry, but next week will be O.K.

A: O.K., I'll tell her. But next week is O.K., you said?
C: Yeah, next week is fine. Listen, I have to run. I have a million things to do.
A: O.K., speak to you soon. Bye.
C: See you.

Conversation 3
A: Hello.
D: Good afternoon. Could I speak to Mrs. Walton, please?
A: She's not here right now. Can I help?
D: It's Mary from AWOL Travel. She knows me. It's just to say that her tickets are ready.
A: Her tickets?
D: Yes, that's right. Her tickets for Mexico City. She can pick them up anytime.
A: Tickets for Mexico City…O.K., I'll tell her.
D: Thanks. Bye.

Conversation 4
A: Hello.
E: Hello, Mrs. Walton?
A: No, this is Dave Walton speaking.
E: Oh, O.K. Could I speak to Mrs. Walton, please?
A: I'm sorry, but she's not in.
E: Oh, I'm calling about her advertisement for a babysitter.
A: Well, uhm, she's not here now.
E: Can I, uh, can she call me back, please?
A: Sure.
E: My name's Amy and my number is 899-5590. Anytime after 6 o'clock tonight.
A: O.K., Amy, I'll tell her. Thanks.
E: Thanks, Mr. Walton. Bye.

Conversation 5
A: Hello.
F: Dave? Hi, it's Brenda. Is Karen there?
A: No, she's at the supermarket, I think.
F: Oh, O.K. Uh, could you do me a favor?
A: Yeah, sure.
F: Well, could you tell her that we have a meeting early tomorrow morning at eight o'clock? At the office. It's with somebody from the legal department, so it's really important that she's there.
A: Eight o'clock tomorrow? I'll tell her.
F: Thanks, Dave. I'll see you this weekend, O.K.?
A: Yeah, see you then. Bye.

Grammar

1 Put the words in the box into the three categories (*verbs*, *nouns*, or *adjectives*) in column A. Then complete column B.

~~agree~~	~~bossy~~	carry	commit	deep
easy	enjoy	~~factory~~	good	illness
hide	hold	kidnap	knife	luxury
messy	rob	roof	rude	run	silly
throw	toe	wide	wife	

A   **B**

verbs   *past participle*

agree   agreed

_____   _____

_____   _____

_____   _____

_____   _____

_____   _____

_____   _____

nouns   *plural*

factory   factories

_____   _____

_____   _____

_____   _____

_____   _____

adjectives   *superlative*

bossy   bossiest

_____   _____

_____   _____

_____   _____

_____   _____

2 Rearrange the words to make questions.

Example
any children Do have you ?
Do you have any children?

a) Do movies James Bond like you ?

_____

_____

b) Are going of out thinking tonight you ?

_____

_____

c) abroad gone Have this year you ?

_____

_____

d) been have here How living long you ?

_____

_____

e) been movies Have recently the to you ?

_____

_____

f) help like me to Would you you ?

_____

_____

3 Each of the sentences below has *one* word missing. Insert the missing words.

Example   to
I'm looking forward/going out tonight.

a) A Che poster pinned on his wall when he was a student.

b) How long you been studying English?

c) I been a DJ for two years.

d) I was wondering you could lend me your car.

e) Is O.K. if I bring my friend?

f) Rosie looking for a new place to live.

g) She kidnapped by a revolutionary group.

Hilda Pagoaga Estrada.

4 Circle the best alternative.

One day in a poor country, a man went to a store to buy some bread. There was a long line, and he spoke to a woman (at) / on the head of the line.

"Excuse me, how long (a) *have you been / you have been* here?"

"Oh, (b) *for / since* about four hours," the woman replied. "They (c) *said / told* us the store would open soon."

The man was in a hurry and decided to ask the woman (d) *help / to help* him. She (e) *looked / was looking* very friendly. "Would you mind (f) *buying / to buy* a loaf of bread for me?" he asked politely.

"I'm sorry, but we're (g) *allow / allowed* to buy only one loaf each," the woman replied.

This is crazy, (h) *thought / was thought* the man. What a country! He decided (i) *going / to go* to the presidential palace. He wanted to (j) *say / tell* the President what he (k) *thought him of / thought of him*. He got out his best suit, (l) *put it on / put on it*, and walked to the palace.

Outside the palace, he (m) *asked / was asked* by a policeman what he wanted.

"I (n) *have been coming / have come* to speak to the President. Could you tell me where (o) *he is / is he*?"

"Certainly," (p) *replied / was replied* the policeman. "(q) *Get / Get in* the line over there. But I have to warn you—the people (r) *at / on* the front (s) *have been waited / have been waiting* (t) *for / since* weeks."

5 Rewrite the sentences, beginning with the words given.

Example
Have you any children?
Do you *have any children?*

a) She told me not to be late.
   She said to me, "_____

   _____

b) President Clinton pardoned her in 2001.
   She was _____

   _____

c) The photo of Che was taken by Alexander Korda.
   Alexander Korda _____

   _____

d) The last time I went to the movies was a month ago.
   I haven't _____

   _____

e) Simone started as a DJ two years ago.
   Simone has _____

   _____

f) Should I call you later?
   Would you _____

   _____

g) Could you take a message?
   I was wondering if _____

   _____

6 Find a response in box B to the sentences in box A.

A

a) Are you having a good time?
b) Come on. Hurry up!
c) Do you have any idea how to send a text message?
d) What was that all about? Why are you getting so angry?
e) Would you like me to pick you up?
f) Would you mind telling her I called?
g) You couldn't lend me $20, could you?
h) You've been working for twelve hours now.

B

1 Calm down. We have plenty of time.
2 Uh, sorry, I'm broke.
3 I've really had enough of him. Why can't he act his age?
4 Of course, no problem. Uh, hold on. Who's calling?
5 So what? It won't kill me.
6 That's all right, thanks. I'll take the bus.
7 To be honest, I don't know much about cell phones.
8 Yeah, great. We're really enjoying ourselves.

Vocabulary

1 Look at the picture and say if each sentence is true (T) or false (F).

Example
A woman is walking down the street with her pet dog. [T]

a) She has wrinkles and false eyelashes. ☐

b) Her hair is straight and dyed blond. ☐

c) She is wearing a fur coat. ☐

d) There are bodyguards on either side of her. ☐

e) Both bodyguards have beards. ☐

f) One of the bodyguards looks like an old hippie. ☐

g) One of the bodyguards is fighting with a protester. ☐

h) There are several protesters on the street. ☐

i) The protesters are demonstrating against fur coats. ☐

j) One protester is pointing at the woman. ☐

k) The woman does not want to take a leaflet. ☐

l) The protesters have put posters on the wall. ☐

m) There is a lot of litter on the street. ☐

2 Complete each sentence with a word from the box. You can use the words more than once.

off   out   over   through   up

Example
We need to find <u>out</u> what time the train leaves.

a) At first she was very sad, but she soon got _____ it.

b) Cheer _____ , Philip! Life isn't that bad!

c) She picked me _____ in the morning, and we went to the demonstration.

d) I tried to speak to him on the phone all day yesterday, but I could never get _____ .

e) She gave _____ smoking on January 1.

f) Students have to turn _____ their cell phones during classes.

g) The demonstration started peacefully, but fighting broke _____ later.

h) The teacher handed _____ the question papers, and the test began.

3 Put the missing words in the grid below to find the hidden word in the gray boxes.

Example
Many people ..... with globalization.

a) We had a great time; we really ..... ourselves.

b) He is a ..... person—always sure of himself.

c) He will ..... a lot of money when his grandmother dies.

d) Tom Cruise ..... in *Mission Impossible*.

e) Her ..... is not serious, but she needs to take a few days off work.

f) ..... vegetables are not treated with chemicals.

g) He had been a very ..... boy, and his parents were angry with him.

	D	I	S	A	G	R	E	E
a)		N					D	
b)		O						T
c)		N				T		
d)		T				D		
e)		L				S		
f)		R				C		
g)		A				Y		

4 Circle the best alternative.

Example
Does he ever (get) / have / make tired of talking?

a) At first I enjoyed it, but then I *got / had / made* bored.
b) He lost his job and quickly *got / had / made* into debt.
c) I *got / had / made* some difficulty with the test.
d) I *got / had / made* an interesting conversation with my boss yesterday.
e) I need to *get / have / make* a phone call to my bank.
f) She *got / had / made* an argument with her boyfriend.
g) The children *get / have / make* very frightened in the dark.
h) The crowd *got / had / made* a lot of noise when the team came onto the field.
i) Why do you always *get / have / make* such a mess?

5 Make nouns from the following words.

Example
confident _____confidence_____

a) cruel _____
b) demonstrate _____
c) difficult _____
d) educate _____
e) explain _____
f) explosive _____
g) inform _____
h) legalize _____
i) mysterious _____
j) pollute _____
k) scientific _____
l) traditional _____

6 Complete each sentence with a noun from exercise 5.

Example
A lot of <u>pollution</u> in cities is caused by traffic.

a) A recent survey showed that most people have no _____ in the government.
b) He completed his _____ at the University of Miami.
c) I'd like some _____ about language courses in San Diego.
d) It was a violent _____ , and there were many arrests.
e) Many politicians now support the _____ of some drugs.

f) The students had no _____ with the exercise and finished quickly.
g) The teacher began the class with an _____ of the grammar rules.
h) They were protesting against _____ to animals.

7 Replace the words in *italics* with their opposites from the box and rewrite the story.

careless	cold	fast	front	narrow
never	rude	unfortunately	violent	wet

It was a *warm*, *dry* day, and we were driving *slowly* down a *wide* street in the town. My husband is a *careful* driver, and he *always* stops at red lights. Suddenly, another car drove into the *back* of our Mercedes. *Fortunately*, my husband is a very *peaceful* man, and he's always very *polite*. He got out of the car…

It was a cold, wet day, and we…

_____
_____
_____
_____
_____
_____
_____
_____
_____
_____

8 Find and correct the twelve spelling mistakes in the story below.

A man went to the dentist for his anual checkup and took a seat in the crowded waiting room. As useual, he was very woried and sat nerviously waiting his turn. Finaly, the receptionist took him in and sat him in the chair.

The dentist carefully examined the man's teeth, turned to the patient, and said, "There's absolutely nothing rong with your teeth. But I would like to ask you to do me a favor."

"Of course," replyed the man.

"I'd like you to screem really loudly—really, really loudly."

"Why?" asked the patient.

"Well, the waiting room is full of poeple who want to see me, and I want to go to a consert this evening."

_____annual_____   _____   _____

_____   _____   _____

_____   _____   _____

_____   _____   _____

16 Lifestyle

Grammar

1 An advertisement for a health spa made the following promises. Insert *will* in an appropriate place in each promise.

> ## After just two weeks with us, …
>
> will
> you lose at least ten pounds.
>
> a) you be relaxed and positive about life.
>
> b) you feel younger and healthier.
>
> c) your energy levels be much higher.
>
> d) relationships with your friends be happier.
>
> e) your general fitness improve.
>
> f) you change the way you think about food.
>
> g) your friends think you look wonderful.

2 A man has made a reservation for two weeks at a health spa.

Do you think the spa will keep its promises? Change four sentences in exercise 1 by
- inserting *probably* or *definitely* and/or
- making the sentences negative to show what you think will happen.

Example
He probably won't lose at least ten pounds.

3 Put each verb into the appropriate form (simple present or *will* + simple verb form).

Example
As soon as he <u>leaves</u> (leave) the spa, he'll have a cigarette.

a) His wife will be happy when he _____ (come) home.

b) If she asks if he liked it, he _____ (say) yes.

c) When it _____ (be) six o'clock, he will go to the neighborhood bar.

d) When his friends see him, they _____ (think) he is sick.

e) He really will be sick if he _____ (lose) any more weight.

f) When he _____ (eat) normally again, he'll put on weight.

g) If his wife _____ (ask) him to go to the health spa again, he'll say no.

4 Put each verb into the appropriate form (simple present or *will* + simple verb form).

Example
When we <u>get</u> (get) to Mexico City, a friend <u>will meet</u> (meet) us in the arrivals area.

a) If he _____ (not be) there, we _____ (take) a taxi.

b) You _____ (have) to speak Spanish if the driver _____ (not speak) English!

c) When we _____ (get) to the hotel, I _____ (call) room service for a bottle of champagne.

d) As soon as we _____ (be) ready, we _____ (look) for a restaurant.

e) We _____ (go) to an expensive restaurant if you _____ (want).

f) If it _____ (not be) too late after dinner, we _____ (find) a place to listen to music.

g) I _____ (tell) you where I got the money when we _____ (get) back to Miami.

Reading

1 Read the article and match the paragraph headings to the paragraphs (A, B, C).

- Genetically Modified Fast Food (*paragraph* ___)
- The Danger to the Environment (*paragraph* ___)
- What is Added to Your Fast Food? (*paragraph* ___)

2 Find the places (1–6) in the article where the following phrases should go.

a) Do you know which chemicals you are eating? ☐

b) Do you want to eat something that has been genetically modified? ☐

c) how much do you know about the fast food you eat? ☐ 1

d) in order to build farms ☐

e) maybe even the cow that the beef comes from ☐

f) Scientists can also make blue potatoes ☐

3 Complete the sentences with words from the article. The paragraph letter is given in parentheses. The first letter of each word has been given to you.

Example
People on Okinawa e x p e c t to live to an old age.

a) What i _ _ _ _ _ _ _ _ _ do I need for this recipe? (A)

b) A diet with lots of fruit and vegetables is good for your h _ _ _ _ _ . (A)

c) R _ _ _ _ _ _ _ shows that there is a connection between smoking and many illnesses. (A)

d) If the p _ _ _ _ _ _ _ _ of fast food is not right, the food will get cold too quickly. (B)

e) The Green Party wants to protect the e _ _ _ _ _ _ _ _ _ _ . (B)

f) Nobody really knows if genetically m _ _ _ _ _ _ _ food is dangerous or not. (C)

TO EAT *or Not to Eat?*

At some time in the future, it is possible that people will look back to our time and remember it as the age of junk food. We all know that there are healthier ways to eat, but that doesn't stop us from spending billions of dollars on hamburgers and hot dogs. But…(1)…

A You should expect to find a lot of chemical ingredients in fast food. None of them are good for your health, but not all of them are bad. Chlorine is used to make bread white. Cochineal (made from dried insects) is used to make things red. However, more research is needed to find out exactly how these chemicals will affect our health in years to come. The question is:…(2)…

B Fast food and packaging come together. When you've eaten the burger, you throw away the packaging and somebody somewhere will then burn or bury it. This is clearly a problem for the environment. Fast food also contributes to global warming. In Brazil, 12 million acres of forest have been cut down…3)…. Farmers use this land to grow soybeans, and the soy is given to the cows that become the beef in your beefburger. Fewer forests = more global warming. The question is: Do you care?

C A lot of fast food contains ingredients that have been genetically modified. The tomatoes in the tomato sauce, the flour in the bread,…(4)…—all of these can be changed by scientists to be very different. How is it possible that you can buy a bright red tomato in Tokyo that comes from Florida and that is still fresh after four weeks? Dutch scientists have grown blue roses.…(5)…. Some of the ideas are strange, but the changes are not always bad. Some plants can be modified to provide more vitamin C, for example. The question is:…(6)…

Vocabulary

1 Complete each question with a word or phrase from the box.

> ~~a diet~~   fit   a healthy life   stress
> vacation   a walk   weight   yoga
> your fitness

Example
Have you ever been on _a diet_ ?

a)   Do you think that you lead _____?

b)   Do you need to improve _____?

c)   What do you do to stay _____?

d)   When did you last go for _____?

e)   Would you like to lose _____?

f)   Have you ever done _____?

g)   How well do you cope with _____?

h)   What do you usually do on _____?

2 Answer each question with a word from the box.

> carrot   chicken   cucumber   eggplant
> garlic   grape   lettuce   ~~peach~~   pepper
> sausage   shrimp   spinach   trout

Example
Which is a fruit that grows on trees? _peach_

a)   Which is a green leaf that contains lots of iron? _____

b)   Which is used to make wine? _____

c)   Which is a river fish? _____

d)   Which lives in the ocean but is not a fish? _____

e)   Which is a vegetable that can be red or green? _____

f)   Which looks like a small onion? _____

g)   Which is orange and grows underground? _____

h)   Which is purple on the outside and white inside? _____

i)   Which is dark green on the outside and pale green inside? _____

j)   Which is a green leaf that is usually used in salads? _____

k)   Which is a bird? _____

l)   Which is made of chopped meat? _____

3 Complete each phrase by matching a verb on the left with a phrase on the right.

a)   baked   1   in a blender
b)   boiled   2   in batter
c)   chopped   3   in a quart of water
d)   eaten   4   very thinly
e)   fried   5   in the oven
f)   broiled   6   into small cubes
g)   mixed   7   on a barbecue
h)   sliced   8   raw

4 Complete each sentence with a word from the box.

> calorie   ~~frozen~~   junk   recipe   snack
> starving   vitamins

Example
It's very easy to cook _frozen_ food in the microwave oven.

a)   He went on a low-_____ diet because he wanted to lose a few pounds.

b)   Many teenagers love _____ food, like french fries and chocolate.

c)   Could you give me the _____ for that dish?

d)   We often have a little _____ between lunch and dinner.

e)   I'm absolutely _____—what time is dinner?

f)   You should eat lots of vegetables to get all the _____ you need.

5 Complete each sentence with an idiom from the box.

> ~~driving me nuts~~   spill the beans
> not my cup of tea   packed in like sardines
> a piece of cake

Example
Stop doing that! It's _driving me nuts_ .

a)   Baseball is very popular in the U.S., but it's _____

b)   The buses are terrible in the morning—you're _____

c)   We finished it in about two seconds—it was _____

d)   It's a big secret, so please don't _____

Writing

Look at the pictures and write the story of Toby's visit to a health spa. Use the questions to help you.

Begin your story like this:
Toby was in bad shape and overweight, and one day his wife gave him a surprise birthday present: one week at a health spa!
When …

Picture 1
What was Toby doing when he arrived at the health spa?
What did the trainer say to him? Why?

Picture 2
How much did Toby weigh on the first morning?
What did his trainer tell him?

Picture 3
When did Toby go to the dining room?
What did he have for lunch?
How did he feel?

Picture 4
What did everybody do in the afternoon?
What happened to Toby?

Picture 5
Who did Toby call that night? Why?
What did he order?
Where did he eat his dinner?
How did he feel?

Picture 6
How much did he weigh at the end of the week? Why?
How did his trainer feel? Why?

Pronunciation

Look at the underlined letters. Which letters in each group of words are pronounced differently? Circle them.

Example
(au)nt   c<u>au</u>liflower   s<u>au</u>sage

a) b<u>ea</u>ns   br<u>ea</u>k   cr<u>ea</u>m
b) h<u>ea</u>lth   h<u>ea</u>ven   p<u>ea</u>ch
c) bel<u>ie</u>ve   fr<u>ie</u>nd   p<u>ie</u>ce
d) n<u>ei</u>ghbor   w<u>ei</u>ght   rec<u>ei</u>ve
e) abr<u>oa</u>d   appr<u>oa</u>ch   t<u>oa</u>st
f) c<u>ou</u>ch   tr<u>ou</u>t   y<u>ou</u>th
g) c<u>ou</u>ntry   m<u>ou</u>ntain   tr<u>ou</u>ble

▭ Listen to the recording to check your answers.

17 *Animals*

Grammar

1 The sentences below were written by schoolchildren on tests. Complete each sentence with a relative pronoun (*who* or *that*). Use *that* only when *who* is not possible.

Example
A fjord is a car <u>that</u> is made in Scandinavia.

a) Charles Darwin was the naturalist _____ wrote *The Organ of the Species*.

b) Electric volts are named after Voltaire, the man _____ invented electricity.

c) Euthanasia is the part of Asia _____ is nearest to Europe.

d) H_2O is water _____ is hot, and CO_2 is cold.

e) Handel was a composer _____ was half German, half Italian, and half English.

f) Karl Marx was a comedian _____ made funny movies with his brothers.

g) The boats _____ are seen in Venice are called gorgonzolas.

h) William Tell is the man _____ invented the telephone.

Can you see what is factually wrong in each sentence?

2 Circle the correct alternative: *that, it, they,* or nothing (–).

Once upon a time, there was a baby camel (*that*)/ *it* lived in a zoo. One day, he turned to his father and said, "Dad, what's the name of this big thing (a) *that / it* is on my back?"

"It's a hump, son," replied the father. "It's a kind of food store (b) *that / it* you need (c) *it / –* when you're in the desert."

"Dad," he said again, "what do you call these hairs (d) *that / they* are above my eyes?"

"They're eyelashes, son. They protect your eyes from the wind that you get (e) *it / –* in the desert," said his dad.

"Dad," he asked, "why do I have feet (f) *that / they* are bigger than all the other animals?"

"The sand (g) *that / it* you get (h) *it / –* in the desert is very soft," said his dad. "Your big feet help you to walk."

"Oh, thanks, Dad," said the baby camel. "So, why do we live in a zoo?"

3 Complete each question with the correct form of the verb in parentheses.

Example
If you <u>saw</u> (see) an injured bird in the street, would you help it?

a) If there were a mosquito in your bedroom, _____ (you try) to kill it?

b) If a cat _____ (come) into your house, would you give it something to eat?

c) If a friend _____ (invite) you to a bullfight, would you go?

d) If you found a spider in the bathtub, what _____ (you do)?

e) If your friends _____ (ask) you to take care of their dog for two weeks, what would you say?

f) If the government closed all the zoos in your country, how _____ (you feel)?

g) If someone asked you to give some money to a hospital for sick animals, how much _____ (you give)?

Now answer the questions so that they are true for you.

Example
Yes, I would. I'd take it to a vet.

_____

_____

_____

_____

_____

_____

_____

_____

Listening

1 📼 Cover the tapescript opposite and listen to a comedian telling jokes about a dog. Put the pictures in the correct order.

a

b

c

d

Have I ever told you about my dog? I never really wanted a dog, but I was in a department store one day last week and I had to go to the top floor where they sell books. I was looking for a good book of jokes. Anyway, I found the escalator, and there was a sign, and it said, "Dogs must be carried." "What do I do?" I thought. "I don't have a dog." Anyway, I found the pet department, which was on the ground floor, and bought myself a dog. You don't want to break the rules, do you? And what a dog! The most intelligent dog I've ever seen. When we got to the book department, there was a sign on the wall. "Wet paint," it said. The dog looked at the sign, barked "woof woof," lifted his leg, and, well, yes, he did. He actually did it right there on the wall. "Wow," I said, "a dog that can read." The dog looked at me and you know what? He spoke! "I can speak, too," he said. This was just too much. A talking dog! I couldn't believe it. I took him back to the pet department, and I said to the man at the counter, I said, "Did you know you have just sold me a dog that can read and talk?" "Yes, I know," said the man, "but he's not very intelligent. When we play chess, I usually win."

The next day I took the dog to an employment office. "Look," I said to the woman there. "I have this dog that can read, do tricks, and talk; he can type sixty words a minute, and he wants a job." The woman looked at me and looked at the dog. "What languages do you speak?" she asked. "Well," said the dog, "I can speak English, and I can speak dog." "Anything else?" asked the woman. "Yes, of course," says the dog. "Meow."

2 📼 Listen again and choose the best answer to each question below.

Example
Why did the man go to the department store?
a) to buy a dog
b) to buy a book ✓

1 Why did he have to take the escalator?
a) because he had a dog
b) because he needed the top floor

2 How did he know that the dog could read?
a) the dog wet the paint
b) the dog told him he could read

3 Why didn't the man in the pet department think the dog was very intelligent?
a) the dog usually lost when they played chess
b) he knew how to play chess

4 Why did the man take the dog to an office?
a) because he wanted a job
b) because he wanted a job for the dog

Vocabulary

1 Search the word square (↑ ↓ → ←) for twenty-four names and classes of animals.

E	O	T	I	U	Q	S	O	M	P	L	H
L	S	D	S	P	I	D	E	R	A	O	S
E	N	O	P	W	B	E	A	R	R	O	I
P	A	L	I	O	R	E	E	D	R	N	F
H	K	P	G	C	C	A	T	E	O	H	E
A	E	H	T	C	E	S	N	V	T	A	S
N	E	I	P	E	N	D	A	I	N	M	E
T	F	N	H	A	T	E	E	H	C	S	L
T	F	F	T	I	E	S	R	O	H	T	T
N	A	L	N	O	C	A	M	E	L	E	R
A	R	O	O	R	A	G	N	A	K	R	U
F	I	D	O	G	I	G	U	A	N	A	T
S	G	R	A	T	E	L	I	T	P	E	R

mosquito   _____   _____

ant   _____   _____

reptile   _____   _____

_____   _____   _____

_____   _____   _____

_____   _____   _____

_____   _____   _____

_____   _____   _____

2 Use the names of the animals in the word square to answer the questions.

Example
Which animal do we get malaria from?

m o s q u i t o

a) Which animal barks? _ _ _
b) Which animal spins a web? _ _ _ _ _ _
c) Which animal is long and sometimes venomous? _ _ _ _ _
d) Which animal carries its baby in a pocket?
   _ _ _ _ _ _ _ _
e) Which animal is a colorful bird?
   _ _ _ _ _ _
f) Which animal eats leaves from the top of trees? _ _ _ _ _ _ _
g) Which animal is the fastest runner?

   _ _ _ _ _ _
h) Which animal do we put a saddle on when we want to ride it? _ _ _ _ _

3 Circle the correct word.

Example
Do you know the fairy *tail* /(*tale*)about the princess and the frog?

a) We had to *wait / weight* two hours for the train.
b) Bambi was a baby *dear / deer*.
c) Why don't you *right / write* him a letter?
d) When we were in the mountains, we saw a huge black *bare / bear*.
e) Gorillas have an average *wait / weight* of about 350 pounds.

4 Choose the best alternative to complete each sentence.

Example
I've always been very <u>interested</u> in reptiles.
fascinated   interested   big

a) I get very _____ with all the animal documentaries on TV.
   bored   interested   worried

b) Are you _____ of snakes?
   afraid   disapprove   fascinated

c) He's really _____ on the idea of going on safari.
   interested   big   thinking

d) Are you _____ about environmental problems?
   interested   tired   worried

e) I had a myna bird, but I got _____ of it talking all the time.
   disapprove   fascinated   tired

f) Do you _____ of keeping animals in zoos?
   approve   think   worry

g) We were _____ by the way the dog did tricks.
   fascinated   bored   tired

h) What do you _____ about getting a hamster as a pet?
   approve   think   interest

Writing

1 Look at the letter below and choose the best pet for Bill from the photos opposite.

> I am a retired manager. I am 74 years old, but I am in very good health. I have been a little lonely since my wife died, and I am sometimes nervous in the house by myself. I live in the country and enjoy going for walks. I don't like cats, but I love all other animals. What pet do you recommend?
>
> *Bill Bowell*

2 Now read the reply below. Does the writer agree with you? Does the writer have the same reasons as you?

> *I am convinced that* the best pet for Bill is a dog.
> *In the first place*, dogs make very good companions, and Bill will be less lonely.
> *Secondly*, Bill enjoys going for walks, so he could take the dog with him. *Finally*, dogs are helpful to protect people in their homes.
> *It seems to me that* hamsters and goldfish are *completely inappropriate*. They do not communicate, and I do not think they will improve Bill's life. A cat is *clearly out of the question because* Bill doesn't like them.
> *In my opinion, therefore*, a dog is *the best choice*. A dog will solve Bill's problems and make him a happier man.

3 Read the letter below and choose the best pet for Zoë.

> I am twelve years old, and I share a room with my twin brother, Arthur. Arthur has a pet mouse, and I want a pet too. I want something cute and cuddly. We live in a twelfth-floor apartment in Manhattan. My parents have agreed to get me a pet, but they have told me that I have to take care of it. They don't like animals, so it has to stay in my room.
>
> *Zoë Houseman*

Write a short reply and explain which pet you think is best for Zoë. Give your reasons.
Use the reply in exercise 2 to help you and use as many of the expressions in *italics* as possible.

Pronunciation

The words in *italics* in each pair of sentences have different pronunciations and different meanings. Decide how to pronounce these words.

1 a) Do you live *close* to the school?
   b) What time does the school *close*?

2 a) They *live* near the TV studios.
   b) There's a *live* concert of U2 on TV tonight.

3 a) Can you show me how to *use* this phone?
   b) It's not much *use*—it doesn't work!

4 a) The *content* of your report is very interesting.
   b) I was *content* to stay home and watch a good movie on TV.

5 a) I really *object* to his behavior.
   b) An intransitive verb does not have an *object*.

6 a) I'm going to visit my *Polish* friend in Warsaw next week.
   b) He likes to *polish* his car every weekend.

📼 Listen to the recording to check your answers.

18 Weird

Grammar

1 Read the sentences. In each case, check (✓) which happened first, a) or b).

Example
It was late when I got home because I had worked late at the office.
a) I got home b) I worked late at the office ✓

1   *I had had a quick dinner and I turned on the TV for the late-night movie,* Alien Killers.
    a) I had dinner b) I turned on the TV

2   *I went to bed as soon as the movie had ended.*
    a) I went to bed b) The movie ended

3   *I saw a bright light at my window after I had gotten into bed.*
    a) I saw a bright light b) I got into bed

4   *I had closed the windows, but there was a strong wind in my room.*
    a) I closed the windows
    b) There was a strong wind

5   *When the wind had gone away, I heard a strange voice.*
    a) The wind went away
    b) I heard a strange voice

6   *When the voice had spoken, the bright light disappeared.*
    a) The voice spoke
    b) The bright light disappeared

2 Make sentences in the past perfect, using the verbs in parentheses.

Example
I felt very ill.
I <u>had eaten</u> (eat) too much.

a)   He looked very pale.
     He _____ (see) a ghost.
b)   She was late for work.
     She _____ (miss) the bus.
c)   She woke up suddenly.
     She _____ (have) a bad dream.
d)   I did very badly on the exam.
     I _____ (not study) very much.
e)   They finally got married.
     They _____ (be engaged) for five years.

3 Circle the correct verb forms.

On July 28, 1900, King Umberto I of Italy (visited) / had visited a restaurant in Monza. He (a) *arrived / had arrived* in the town earlier that day. He had his dinner and then (b) *spoke / had spoken* to the restaurant owner, also named Umberto. He (c) *discovered / had discovered* that they (d) *were / had been* born in the same town on the same day. The king introduced his wife, whose name (e) *was / had been* Margherita. The name of the restaurant owner's wife (f) *was / had been* Margherita, too. They then (g) *discovered / had discovered* another amazing coincidence. Both couples (h) *got married / had gotten married* on the same day, more than 30 years previously.

The day after their meeting, the king was very sad to learn that the restaurant owner (i) *died / had died* in a shooting accident. He was turning to his assistant to ask about the funeral when he (j) *heard / had heard* a shot from a gun. King Umberto died instantly—the victim of an assassination.

4 Put each verb in parentheses into the correct form (simple past or past perfect).

In 1887, Lucy Dodson <u>was</u> (be) in bed when she (a) _____ (hear) a voice call her name. She (b) _____ (realize) that it was the voice of her mother, who (c) _____ (die) 16 years previously. She (d) _____ (look) up and saw that her mother was carrying two small children in her arms. The ghost (e) _____ (ask) Lucy to take care of the children because they (f) _____ (lose) their mother. Lucy (g) _____ (take) the children into her bed, but when she woke up in the morning, the bed was empty and the children (h) _____ (leave). Two days later, Lucy learned that her sister-in-law (i) _____ (die) that same night, leaving two small children. She later (j) _____ (discover) that her mother's ghost had appeared to her just two hours after her sister-in-law's death.

Reading

1 Match the paragraph beginnings 1–6 with the paragraph endings a–f opposite to tell the story. The paragraph beginnings are in the correct order.

1 One morning in March 1889, a man named Ansel Bourne woke up feeling confused. …

2 "Good morning, Mr. Brown," said the people in the stationery store. …

3 "Go and get Mr. Brown a chair," said a man in the store. …

4 When the reply arrived, everybody was shocked. …

5 Two months earlier, on January 17, Mr. Ansel Bourne had left his home early in the morning. …

6 For two months, Bourne's family in Greene had tried to find him. …

2 Read the story again and put the events below in the order in which they happened.

a) He arrived in a town 200 miles from his home.
b) He asked the people to call his family.
c) He disappeared.
d) He returned to his old life.
e) He went to a bank and took out some money.
f) He went to work in a stationery store.
g) He woke up one morning and felt very confused.
h) People that he didn't recognize said "Good morning" to him.

1	2	3	4	5	6	7	8
e							d

Mr. Bourne or Mr. Brown?

a … "He's not feeling well." Mr. Bourne told them his name again and asked them to contact his family in Greene. The staff in the store wanted to keep him happy, so they sent a telegram to Greene.

b … By March, everybody thought that thieves had killed him and stolen the money that he had taken out of the bank. Bourne returned home to his old life. He had no memory of the day he had disappeared, and he was never able to explain why he had gone to Pennsylvania.

c … He had gone to the bank, taken some money out of his account, and immediately disappeared. A few days later Mr. A.J. Brown arrived in Norristown and bought a stationery store on the main street. It was the same man.

d … He was in a strange bed in a strange apartment. How had he gotten there? He had no idea. He knew his name and that he lived in Greene, Rhode Island, but that was all he knew. He got up, got dressed, had breakfast, and walked down the street to a stationery store. He wasn't really sure why, but he felt that he had to go there. He found that he was in the town of Norristown, Pennsylvania, 200 miles from Greene.

e … They seemed to know him, but he had never seen them before. He told them that his name was Bourne. They thought he was joking, but it was soon clear that he was being serious.

f … The man was really Ansel Bourne, and his family had almost given up hope of finding him again. But for two months, the people of Norristown had known him as Mr. Brown, the owner of the stationery store on their main street.

Vocabulary

1 Complete each question with a word from the box.

> far ~~fast~~ long many much often
> old well

Example

How _fast_ can you drive on highways in your country?

a) How _____ people are there in your class?

b) How _____ is the youngest student in your class?

c) How _____ do you know your teacher?

d) How _____ does your teacher give you homework?

e) How _____ does it take you to get to school?

f) How _____ is your home from your school?

g) How _____ did you pay for this book?

Now answer the questions.

2 Complete each sentence with *have*, *make*, or *take*.

Example

People say that teachers and doctors _have_ lots in common.

a) A professional photographer came to _____ pictures of the wedding.

b) He's going to _____ a course in business English.

c) Her secretary will _____ all the travel arrangements.

d) I _____ no idea what causes crop circles.

e) She doesn't _____ any experience in the travel industry.

f) Ladies and gentlemen, please _____ your seats.

g) They hope to _____ a lot of money with their new company.

h) This government does not _____ promises that it cannot keep.

3 Complete each sentence with a word or phrase from the box.

> embarrassed excited ~~exhausted~~
> frightened in a bad mood jealous
> on top of the world proud sad

Example

He had run more than six miles, and he was _exhausted_.

a) He was _____ because she went to see her old boyfriend.

b) I was so _____ when I forgot his name.

c) I'm _____ because I had a lot of problems at work today.

d) It was the first time he had run a marathon, and he was very _____ of himself.

e) Many people were very _____ when they heard that the princess had died.

f) She had a lovely family, wonderful friends, and a fantastic job, and she was _____ .

g) There was only one more day before the party and the children were feeling very _____ .

h) We were lost in a dark forest, and we were very _____ .

4 Complete the story by changing the verbs in parentheses to nouns.

Government officials are investigating the _disappearance_ (disappear) of a top secret spy plane during a training (a) _____ (fly) last week. Colonel Vance Arkin of the U.S. Air Force, who is leading the (b) _____ (investigate), says there are a number of possible (c) _____ (explain). One theory is that the plane did not have (d) _____ (permit) to fly over a nuclear testing site in Nevada, controlled by the U.S. Army, and that it was shot down. However, the army says that it has no record in its radar log of a plane that matches the (e) _____ (describe) of the spy plane. The Air Force has spent billions of dollars on the (f) _____ (develop) of this plane, and officials are worried that this accident will damage public (g) _____ (confide) in the project.

Writing

Complete the story. Answer the questions and use your imagination.

THE WEATHER WAS BAD ON THE DAY OF THE FUNERAL. THERE WAS ONLY ONE PERSON THERE, AND HE HAD PUT A SINGLE ROSE ON THE COFFIN...

Who had died? When? How had he/she died?
Who was the man at the funeral? Why was he there?
Why had nobody else come to the funeral?

NOBODY IS TOO SURE ABOUT EXACTLY WHAT HAPPENED. WHEN THE POLICE ARRIVED, THEY SAW...

What did the police see when they arrived?
Where was the spaceship shining its light?
What had happened to the man with the dark glasses?

THREE THOUSAND LIGHT YEARS AWAY, AN ALIEN HAD JUST ARRIVED AT A PARTY.

Where was the party?
Why was everybody happy at the party?
What happened next?

Pronunciation

Read and listen to the mini-dialogue below.

– *We have Ben Crystal with us here in the studio.*
– *Sorry, my name is **Ken** Crystal.*

The word *Ken* is stressed because it is the most important word in the sentence.

Look at the following mini-dialogues and decide which word (or words) is stressed in the second lines.

a) – Ken, you say you've visited many crop circles.
   – Yes, I've seen about a thousand.

b) – When were the first crop circles reported?
   – The first crop circle was seen in 1980.

c) – What time yesterday afternoon did you find the circle?
   – Actually, we found it in the morning.

d) – Do you think this crop circle was caused by the weather?
   – No, we think it was made by aliens.

e) – This circle is very big, isn't it?
   – Yes, it's about a half a mile wide!

f) – Is this crop circle like all the others?
   – No, I've never seen one like this.

Listen to the recording to check your answers.

19 *Wheels*

Grammar

1 In the sentences below, replace the simple past with *used to* + simple verb form **where it is possible**.

Example
As a child, I rode my bike to school every day.
As a child, I used to ride my bike to school every day.

a) The roads were quiet and safe.

_____

b) My parents gave me a racing bike for my tenth birthday.

_____

c) I was very proud of my bike.

_____

d) I cleaned it every day.

_____

e) My best friend was a boy named Tom.

_____

f) One day, I lent him my bike.

_____

g) He gave it back to me a week later.

_____

h) One wheel was broken, and it was all dirty.

_____

2 Rearrange the words to make suggestions for and give advice to a person who is going to study English in Miami.

Example
a club don't join health there Why you
Why don't you join a health club there?

a) a choose good I I'd If language school were you

_____
_____

b) a could for job look there You

_____
_____

c) an don't American family stay Why with you

_____
_____

d) go I I'd If in the were winter you

_____
_____

3 Write five sentences with *used to/didn't use to* + simple verb form comparing city life now and city life at the beginning of the 20th century. You can use the pictures to help you.

Examples
There used to be horses on the street.
People didn't use to drive to work.

_____
_____
_____
_____
_____
_____

Listening

1 📼 Cover the tapescript opposite and listen to three people talking about their dream cars. Match the speaker to the cars.

2 📼 Which of the topics below do the speakers discuss? Listen again and put a check (✓) or an ex (✗) next to the topics for each speaker.

	Speaker 1	Speaker 2	Speaker 3
What color is it?	✗		
What special features does it have?	✓		
How fast does it go?			
Where would you like to go in your car?			
Who would you take with you?			

Speaker 1

I've always wanted one of those, what do you call them, those recreational vehicle things. You know, an RV. We'd need four beds, for the two of us and the grandchildren. Those RVs all have little kitchens and a dining table, and most of them even have a john, you know, a toilet. A television would be nice for the children. I think I'd probably like to make my own curtains and things like that. We could take the grandchildren to Michigan with us in the summer, and they could visit the whole family.

Speaker 2

My dream car is a huge white stretch limo. You know, one of those really, really long ones, the size of a bus. It has to be pure white, with black windows that no one can look through, and shiny chrome wheels. And a chauffeur, of course. I don't want to drive it myself. Brad Pitt is the chauffeur. Or maybe his brother if he looks like him. Inside there's room for all my friends, with a cocktail bar and a large screen DVD and things like that. And a sunroof, because we'll drive around Hollywood and everyone will look at us and want to know who we are. Hmm, no, they won't be able to see us with the dark windows, will they? Oh well, we could always open the windows…

Speaker 3

I've always wanted a really fast sports car. There's a McLaren Formula 1, and it can do nearly 250 miles an hour. That would be cool. Yeah, a brand new, bright red McLaren with the world's most powerful car stereo, and I could listen to all my CDs. Can you imagine driving a thing like that? Top speed around the streets of Monte Carlo. Is it Monte Carlo where they do that 24-hour race? Anyway, Monte Carlo sounds cool. Jennifer Lopez in the passenger seat and the stereo on full blast. But maybe not Jennifer Lopez's music…You need something heavier, some hard rock.

3 📼 Either listen again or look at the tapescript and write answers to the questions in the chart in exercise 2.

Vocabulary

1 Complete each sentence with a word from the box.

> belts   hood   ~~bumper~~   engine   gears
> seats   steering   tire   trunk   windshield
> wipers

Example
Cars have a <u>bumper</u> at the front and the back for
protection in an accident.

a) A driver has to take one hand off the
_____ wheel to change _____ .

b) All cars have safety _____ for the
front _____ , and new cars have them
in the back, too.

c) In most cars, the _____ is under the
_____ at the front of the car.

d) Many cars have a spare _____ in the
_____ .

e) When it's raining, you need to turn on the
_____ _____ .

2 Combine a word from box A with a word from
box B to make a compound noun. Then complete
the sentences with the compound nouns.

A

> air
> ~~down~~
> driver's
> fast
> hair
> health
> public
> summer
> traffic

B

> care
> food
> conditioning
> ~~town~~
> vacation
> jam
> license
> style
> transportation

Example
It's very difficult to park <u>downtown</u>.

a) _____ in the city is
excellent, with good buses and a fast subway
system.

b) All the rooms in the hotel have
_____ .

c) I almost didn't recognize her with her new
_____ .

d) I'm sorry I'm late—there was a huge
_____ on the highway.

e) Many traditional restaurants have closed
because more and more people are eating
_____ .

f) My new company has excellent employee
benefits—with a really good
_____ plan.

g) The school is closed during the
_____ .

h) You have to take a test before you get a
_____ .

3 Complete each sentence with an adverb from the
box.

> abroad   casually   closely   dangerously
> heavily   intelligently   ~~occasionally~~
> partly   specially

Example
He <u>occasionally</u> cooks for his friends.

a) He was driving _____ , and the
police stopped him.

b) I admit I was _____ to blame for
the accident.

c) It was raining _____ this morning.

d) People dress very _____ in the office
where she works—jeans and running shoes.

e) She _____ resembles her mother—
people often think they are sisters.

f) The article was _____ written, but
it was hard to understand.

g) The car was _____ designed for
driving in cities.

h) We usually go _____ for our
vacations.

4 Make adjectives from the nouns in parentheses.

The new model is <u>economical</u> (economy) to run
but has a (a) _____ (power) 2.4-liter
engine. It has a (b) _____ (space)
interior and an (c) _____ (electricity)
sunroof for summer driving.
* * * *
Some of our large cities are (d) _____
(pollution) and crowded. But now there is
another problem, with more and more
(e) _____ (aggression) drivers on
the roads. Many drivers seem to be less
(f) _____ (consideration) than
they used to be, and some people get
(g) _____ (anger) for no reason at all.
To be (h) _____ (safety), it is probably
(i) _____ (wisdom) to lock your doors
and keep the windows closed.

Writing

1 Read the letter opposite. What is the purpose of the letter?

- to give advice about renting a car
- to give advice about traveling in Florida
- to give some personal news

2 Draw the itinerary that Penny suggests on the map.

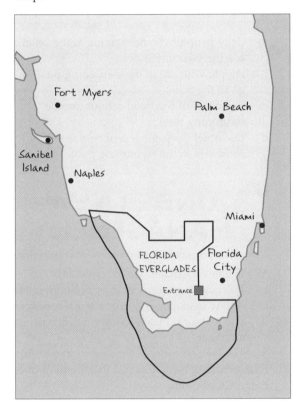

3 Underline in the letter opposite all the ways that Penny gives advice and makes suggestions. An example has been done for you.

4 Look at this extract from a letter.

> It was very nice of you to invite me to come and stay with you. I have a really cheap flight. It arrives a week before your vacation starts, so I thought that I would spend a week traveling around by car. I'll come and see you after that. Do you have any good ideas? Where should I go?

Use Penny's letter opposite as a model and reply to the letter above.

Dear Elena,

 Many thanks for your letter. It was good to hear from you, and it is fantastic news that you're coming to Florida. I think that it's a really good idea for you to spend a week traveling around the state before coming to see me.

 If I were you, I'd rent a car. There's really no other way to go. I suggest that you drive north from Miami to Palm Beach. The Flagler Museum there is great! You could visit Elaine while you're there. The next day, you could drive west to Fort Myers and visit the Thomas Edison Museum. You'll love it!

 I know you like the beach, so why don't you go to Sanibel Island? The beach is wonderful, and there aren't too many tourists. After that, drive south to Naples, an interesting city. From Naples, drive southeast across the state to Florida City. Everglades National Park is ten miles west of Florida City. You probably won't have time for anything else, but when you're back in Miami, we can get together and visit a few more places.

 Anyhow, that's all for now. I hope I've given you a few ideas. I'll write again very soon.

Love,
Penny

Pronunciation

1 🔲 Listen to two people speaking.

Which speaker sounds more positive? Which speaker uses a higher tone of voice?

2 🔲 Listen to the recording and practice saying the sentences in a positive way.

a) I think my classes are a lot of fun.
b) The school I go to is excellent.
c) My English has really improved this year.
d) My teacher is the best in the world.

20 *Review 4*

Grammar

1 Look at the sign in each question and choose the best explanation.

❶

> Closed for lunch
> Back at 3:00

a) You can come back for lunch at 3 o'clock.
b) They will have lunch at 3 o'clock.
c) The shop will close after 3 o'clock.
d) The shop will open at 3 o'clock.

❷

> **WE NO LONGER ACCEPT CREDIT CARDS**
> Sorry for any inconvenience

a) They are going to accept credit cards soon.
b) They will only accept credit cards.
c) They used to accept credit cards.
d) They are sorry that the credit cards are very long.

❸

> *Jacket and tie required*
> **NO SNEAKERS OR T-SHIRTS**

a) People who are wearing jackets and ties cannot come in.
b) People who are wearing sneakers or T-shirts cannot come in.
c) You have to wear sneakers or a T-shirt with your jacket.
d) You can wear anything you want.

❹

> **Insert key card, wait for green light, and immediately push down door handle**

a) Do not insert the key card when you push down the door handle.
b) Push the door handle as soon as you see the green light.
c) Insert the key card after you see the green light.
d) Push the key card into the door immediately.

❺

> **SEAVIEW** HOTEL
> THIS SWIMMING POOL IS FOR THE USE OF RESIDENTS ONLY

a) Only people who are staying at the hotel can use the swimming pool.
b) People who are in the swimming pool must go to the hotel.
c) Residents of the hotel cannot use the swimming pool.
d) The hotel does not accept responsibility for accidents in the swimming pool.

❻

> **UNDER NEW MANAGEMENT**

a) The new manager has recently left.
b) The new management does not understand.
c) A new manager is going to work here soon.
d) The restaurant used to have a different manager.

2 Each sentence has one word that should not be there. Cross it out.

Example
Could you explain ~~me~~ how to send an e-mail?

a) We will take a break when we will finish this exercise.
b) That's the man I told you about him.
c) I have a friend who she got married last week.
d) They were used to live in Monterrey.
e) If you read more books, your English it would improve.
f) I would to see a doctor if I were you.
g) I hope I will to find a good job soon.
h) When he had finished breakfast, he had left for work.
i) She used to have wearing long blond hair.
j) Why don't you speak to someone who he understands the problem?

3 Rewrite the sentences, beginning with the words given.

Example
We're not allowed to smoke in the office.
We cannot *smoke in the office.*

a) Alex said, "If I were you, I'd review Unit 17."
Alex said, "Why don't _____
_____

b) The first student to finish will receive a prize.
The student who _____
_____

c) I'll finish my work, and then I'll help you.
When I _____
_____

d) She peeled the potato and then sliced it.
When she had _____
_____

e) I'll give you a call when our train arrives.
As soon as _____
_____

f) My friend has invited me to visit—he lives in L.A.
My friend who _____
_____

g) A few years ago, this was a green field.
A few years ago, this used _____
_____

4 Find a response in box B for the sentences in box A.

A

a) Are you in love with him?
b) But when will I find time?
c) Should I tell him what I think?
d) Do you think you'll pass your exams?
e) Don't you think this is kind of boring?
f) Is there anything good on TV tonight?
g) What do you think of the new teacher?
h) When will you pay me back?
i) Why didn't you get a taxi?

B

1 Well, I'm not very big on her.
2 As soon as I get to the bank.
3 I didn't have enough cash on me.
4 I hope so.
5 I wouldn't if I were you.
6 No, but I used to be.
7 No, nothing special.
8 Well, you could take a day off work.
9 Yes, I'm sick of it.

5 Fill each blank with one word only.

You _have_ probably never heard of John Montagu, but he has another name (a) _____ is famous around the world. John Montagu, Earl of Sandwich, used (b) _____ spend a lot of his time playing cards. In fact, one day (c) _____ 1762, he played for more (d) _____ 24 hours without stopping. He wanted something that (e) _____ could eat while he (f) _____ playing. He (g) _____ given some meat and cheese between two slices (h) _____ bread. This meal became known (i) _____ the "sandwich." However, the sandwich is not the only thing (j) _____ carries his name. The Hawaiian Islands in the Pacific (k) _____ to be called the Sandwich Islands and were named (l) _____ the famous card player. It is perhaps surprising (m) _____ he was honored in this way. (n) _____ the time, Sandwich was the British Foreign Minister, and many people thought that he (o) _____ responsible for losing the American Revolution.

Vocabulary

1 Choose the best alternative from the options below to fill in each blank.

Casanova will always be <u>famous</u> for his success with the (a) _____ sex, but few people really know much about this extraordinary (b) _____. He was born in 1725, and when he was sixteen he began a (c) _____ in the church. However, the church (d) _____ of his wild (e) _____ , and he left Venice and the church.

    In 1749, his (f) _____ with Henriette began. It was one of the most important in his life, and it (g) _____ six months before they (h) _____ . At this time, he developed a strong (i) _____ of friends who helped him return to Venice. He was soon in (j) _____ again, and for a (k) _____ , he was in prison. He managed to (l) _____ to France, where he worked as a secret agent and was one of the founders of the first national lottery.

    A life that was full of excitement and embarrassing (m) _____ followed. He traveled throughout Europe and (n) _____ ended up in Dux, in the Czech Republic, where he died in 1798.

Example

(famous)   good-looking   gorgeous

a) different   equal   opposite
b) ancestor   character   hamster
c) career   employer   profession
d) afraid   disapproved   worried
e) diet   lifestyle   meditation
f) girlfriend   partner   relationship
g) consisted   had   lasted
h) bored   exhausted   separated
i) network   schedule   web
j) problem   surprise   trouble
k) pause   run   while
l) arrange   escape   risk
m) incidents   intelligence   interiors
n) awfully   eventually   heavily

2 Complete the story with words from the box.

about	as	at	for	in	of	to	with

Janet Rose was fed up <u>with</u> her job as a waitress at a pizzeria in Manhattan. She was sick (a) _____ doing the same thing every day, and she wanted to have an experience (b) _____ something new. She had thought (c) _____ taking a course in restaurant management, but she couldn't give (d) _____ her job, because she needed the money.

    One day, her favorite customer walked in. He was old enough to be her grandfather, but they had lots (e) _____ common, and they often chatted. That evening, the old man ate his pizza (f) _____ usual, but he didn't seem interested (g) _____ talking. (h) _____ fact, he seemed to be very worried (i) _____ something. When he left, Janet went to clear his table. (j) _____ her surprise, she found a piece of paper under his plate. She picked it up and read: "Dear Janet, I hope you will not object (k) _____ this present. You remind me (l) _____ my darling wife, and I have always been very fond (m) _____ you. All my love, Alan Lawson." She turned over the paper and saw that it was a check for $150,000.

    Janet was unable (n) _____ thank him (o) _____ his present. She tried to call him on the phone, but there was no reply. He had died (p) _____ a heart attack (q) _____ his way home from the restaurant.

3 Complete each sentence by making an adjective from the word in parentheses.

Example
He's a <u>dangerous</u> (danger) driver.

a) Male animals are often more _____ (aggression) than females.
b) They were not _____ (amusement) when they lost $100,000.
c) Why do you get _____ (anger) every time I make a mistake?
d) How _____ (belief) do you find the stories about crop circles?
e) She has a _____ (jealousy) husband, and she can't go out.
f) The car had leather seats and a _____ (space) interior.
g) His exam grades were extremely _____ (surprise).

4 Replace the words in *italics* with their opposites from the box and rewrite the story.

> awful   failure   forgot   full   little
> nervous   previous   shy   silly   ~~unlucky~~
> weak

Maggie was always *lucky* with men, and one day she contacted a computer dating service. She was looking for a *strong* personality because she was very *outgoing* herself. A week later, the dating service found a man. They said he had *lots* in common with her and they were sure their first date would be a *success*.

Before going out, Maggie *remembered* to brush her teeth and put on her new perfume. She smelled *great*! Feeling really *confident*, she arrived at the restaurant, which was almost *empty*. Then, she saw him, sitting at a table with a *serious* expression on his face. It was definitely him. It was her *future* husband!

Maggie was always unlucky with men …

---

5 Complete the crossword. You have seen all the words that you need in Units 16–19 of *American Inside Out*. Some of the letters have been given to you.

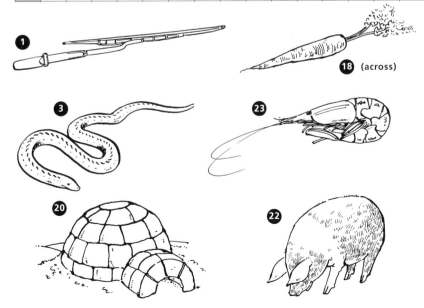

1 (pen/stick illustration)

18 (across) (carrot illustration)

3 (snake illustration)

23 (shrimp illustration)

20 (tortoise illustration)

22 (pig illustration)

Clues

Across
1 see picture 1 (10, 5)
6 I'm trying to follow a ___-calorie diet. (3)
8 A vet ___ sick animals. (6)
9 what we do in a restaurant (3)
10 past tense of 9 across (3)
11 in a foreign country (6)
14 make; for example, to ___ a crop circle (6)
15 place to record music or make movies (6)
16 see; pay attention to (6)
18 see picture 18 (6)
19 He's a bad student; he ___ ___ his homework (4, 2)
21 animal hair (3)
22 see picture 22 (3)
23 see picture 23 (6)
24 put two numbers together (3)
25 system for keeping a building cold (15)

Down
2 what we can say if we want to disagree with someone (1, 4, 5, 2)
3 see picture 3 (5)
4 salad plant (7)
5 not alive (4)
7 what we send using e-mail (7)
12 ___ rage: anger between car drivers (4)
13 quickly and without warning (3, 2, 1, 6)
15 weird (7)
17 If ___ ___ $1,000,000, I'd buy a yacht. (1, 3)
18 cut into small pieces (past tense) (7)
19 is going to (4)
20 see picture 20 (5)

Answer key

1 Me

Grammar

1
1. What   Coppola
2. Which   Ringo Starr
3. Where   London
4. When   1997

2
a) Did you argue
b) Is that
c) Do you like
d) is your favorite Beatles song?
e) Do you think

3
a) How much *do* you weigh?
b) (no change)
c) How often *does* your teacher give you homework?
d) What *did* you have for breakfast today?
e) (no change)
f) (no change)

4
a) Why did David Bowie's son change his name?
b) Who named his daughter after a section of London?
c) How many languages does A.L.I.C.E. speak?
d) When did John Lennon record *Stand By Me*?

Answers
a) Because it was embarrassing.
b) Ex-US President Bill Clinton.
c) Only English.
d) 1975.

Reading

1
a) The world's most inappropriate name
b) Will you marry me?
c) How stupid can you be?

2 a) 4   b) 1   c) 2   d) 3   e) 6   f) 5

3 *Suggested answers*
a) How many legs did the dog have?
b) What did the dog have around its neck?
c) What was Sir Thomas Beecham's job? / What did Sir Thomas Beecham do?
d) Which name couldn't Sir Thomas Beecham change?
e) When did they get married?
f) Where did Mrs. Smith see the names?
g) When did she discover her terrible mistake?

Vocabulary

1 a) Mary   b) Mimi   c) Yoko   d) Julia   e) Yuka

2 a) True   b) True   c) False   d) False   e) False
f) False   g) True   h) False

3
a) correct   b) correct
c) They looked ~~like~~ a little tired after the lesson.
d) correct
e) She sounds ~~like~~ foreign—is she Greek?
f) correct
g) You look ~~like~~ stressed out. What's up?

4 a) 4   b) 7   c) 1   d) 3   e) 8   f) 2   g) 6   h) 5

5 a) used-car salesman   b) doctor
c) police officer   d) banker   e) waiter
f) psychologist   g) student   h) nanny

Writing

1 Message a)   languages, communicating, people
Message b)   favorite (*or* favourite (UK)), team, address
Message c)   country, beautiful, beach
Message d)   especially, writing, homework
Message e)   improve, different, receiving

Pronunciation

1 mean – niece – feel   movie – improve – grew
thoughts – call – daughter   world – learn – girl

2 a) part   b) wheel/we'll   c) tool   d) first
e) born

2 Place

Grammar

1 *Plurals ending in "s"*
statues taxis tourists

Plurals ending in "es"
brushes churches watches

Plurals ending in "ies"
qualities summaries universities

Irregular plurals
men teeth women

2 a) progress   b) luggage   c) homework
d) information   e) money   f) bread   g) air

3 a) much   b) much   c) much   d) many
e) much   f) many   g) many
Students' own answers

4 a) much   b) a little – False (It can get a lot of snow in the winter.)   c) many – False (Many people speak languages other than English.)
d) a few – False (Almost all police officers carry guns.)   e) a few – False (The mayor makes speeches many times each year.)
f) many – True   g) much – False (There is a lot of modern architecture in New York.)
h) much – False (You can see a lot of traffic downtown.)

Listening

1 Picture b

2
  a) False – He first went to Marrakech ten to twelve years ago.
  b) False – He went there for a (long) weekend.
  c) False – He traveled with his best friend, Dave.
  d) True
  e) False – After dinner, he went to the market square.
  f) False – Djemaa el Fna is the name of the market square.
  g) True
  h) True
  i) False – He has been there ten or twelve times.
  j) False – His last visit was three years ago.

Vocabulary

1 a) statue b) beach c) square d) office building
   e) castle f) hill g) church h) fountain

2

things you like	things you don't like
spectacular	ugly
amazing	awful
lovely	disgusting
attractive	dull
exciting	miserable
fabulous	terrible
fantastic	useless
great	

3 a) French b) Japanese c) Hungarian d) Irish
   e) Italian f) Portuguese g) Egyptian
   h) Argentinian

4 a) in b) in c) on d) in e) on f) at g) in

Pronunciation

Oo	oO
enter	decide
happen	describe
label	discuss
listen	explain
mention	relax
practice	repeat
visit	suppose

Writing

1 Dear <u>Mom and Dad,</u>
I got here <u>a few days ago</u>, and I'm having a <u>fabulous</u> time. The weather is <u>terrible</u>, but there are <u>lots</u> of things to do. There are a few <u>places of interest</u> near the hotel where I <u>go in the afternoon</u> and <u>take pictures</u>. I've met a <u>professor of archeology</u> from <u>Brasília</u> who is taking me to <u>some interesting ruins</u> tomorrow. The <u>food</u> is interesting—so different from at home. I'm always really tired in the <u>evening</u> after so much <u>sightseeing</u>—I'll need a vacation after this!
<u>Love,</u>
Barry

3 Couples

Grammar

1 a) met b) fell c) forgot d) were e) wanted
   f) killed g) thought h) was i) woke
   j) found k) took l) killed

2
  a) Where did Romeo meet Juliet? / Where did Romeo and Juliet meet?
  b) Who did Romeo forget about?
  c) Who did Juliet's family want her to marry?
  d) Who did Romeo kill?
  e) Why did Romeo kill himself?
  f) What did Juliet do when she woke up? / What happened when she woke up?
  g) How did Juliet kill herself?

3 a) was holding b) was feeling c) was sitting
   d) was hoping e) were talking
   f) was making g) was getting

4 a) was watching b) said
   c) opened d) was sitting
   e) began f) wanted g) was raining
   h) decided i) arrived

Reading

1 1 B 2 D 3 C 4 A

2

1	2	3	4	5	6	7	8	9	10	11	12
d	h	c	l	a	g	i	k	j	e	b	f

3 *Suggested answers*
  a) She met Onassis.
  b) Because he treated her like a woman.
  c) Because he was seeing other women.
  d) She was reading the newspaper. / She saw it / read about it in the newspaper.
  e) Because his marriage was not happy.
  f) She was visiting Onassis's grave.

Vocabulary

1

1	2	3	4	5	6	7	8	9
a	c	e	i	b	g	d	h	f

2 a) dream b) marriage c) unfaithful d) lover
   e) rumors f) affair g) divorced

3 a) have b) have c) have d) have e) get
   f) get g) get

4 a) out b) up c) out d) out e) up f) up
   g) out

Pronunciation

1 a) begun b) drank c) ran d) rung e) sung
   f) sank g) swum

2 a) /rid/ b) /rɛd/ c) /rɛd/

4 Fit

Grammar

1 a) happier b) hotter c) more successful
d) better e) more interesting f) bigger
g) worse

2 Rosa Jake Lizzie Daniel David

3 a) The biggest b) The luckiest c) The highest
d) the most expensive e) the driest
f) the richest g) the longest

4 Probably the *most* common health problem for men
is heart disease. Exercise is important, but not *as*
important as a healthy diet. A bad diet is *the* biggest
cause of this disease. Vegetables are better for you *than*
fatty foods, but some vegetables are *more* useful than
others. Supermarket products are *not* as healthy as
organic produce. People with *the* most stressful jobs
have shorter lives *than* people who are stress-free, so
look for ways to relax. You should exercise more *than*
once a week. A hard, sweaty sport is not *as* good
for you *as* regular, gentle exercise.

Listening and reading

1 Picture a) Story 2
Picture b) Story 3
Picture c) Story 1

2 a) EE b) SK c) EE d) EM e) SK
f) EM g) SK h) EE i) EM j) SK, EE

3 1 a) 2 a) 3 b) 4 a) 5 b) 6 b)

Vocabulary

1 a) boxing b) swimmer c) gymnast
d) ice hockey player e) rower f) skiing
g) racquetball

2 a) goes b) does c) does d) plays e) does
f) goes g) goes h) plays i) goes

3 a) fortunate b) calm c) attractive d) fit
e) average f) fun g) famous

4 a) Professional b) sweaty c) aerobic
d) dangerous e) talented f) successful
g) valuable

5 a) 6 b) 3 c) 7 d) 1 e) 4 f) 5 g) 2

Writing

1 A man was feeling sick, and he went to see the
doctor. He went with his wife because he was a
little worried. Afterwards the doctor spoke to the
man's wife. He said, "I'm afraid I have some bad
news. Unless you follow my instructions very
carefully, your husband will die. Every morning
you must give him a good breakfast, and you
must cook him a healthy meal at night. What's
more, you must not ask him to do any housework,
and you must keep the house very clean. It is a
lot of work for you, but it really is the only way
to keep him alive."

On the way home, the husband asked his
wife what the doctor had said to her. "He said
you're going to die," she replied.

2 One day a *bus* driver was in his *bus* when the
biggest man he had ever seen got on. The giant
looked at the driver, said, "Big John *doesn't* pay,"
and took his *seat* on the *bus*. The *bus* driver was
only a *little* man, and he did not want to argue.

The next day, the same thing *happened*. The
man mountain got on the *bus*, looked at the
driver, and said, "Big John *doesn't* pay." Then he
went to a seat.

This *happened* for *several* days. After a *week*,
the driver was *beginning* to get a *little* angry.
Everybody else *paid*, so why not the big man?
So the driver went to a gym and began a course
of *bodybuilding*. He did not want to be
frightened of Big John anymore.

Two *weeks* later, the driver had strong
muscles and was *feeling* very fit. At the usual
stop, Big John got on. "Big John *doesn't* pay," he
said. But this time the driver was *prepared* for
him. He got up and said, "Oh, yeah? And why
doesn't Big John pay?"

The man reached into his *pocket*. For a
moment, the driver was *extremely* scared.
Perhaps he had a gun. Then the man *replied*,
"Because Big John has a *bus* pass."

Pronunciation

1 1 a) 2 b) 3 b) 4 c) 5 b) 6 c) 7 a)

2

Ooo	oOo
advertise	attractive
certainly	opinion
cheeseburger	percentage
marathon	statistics
photograph	surprising
tournament	
wonderful	

---

5 Review 1

Grammar

1 The Key gives the parts of speech of the words as
they are used in Units 1–4.

verbs	past tense
become	became
catch	caught
choose	chose
draw	drew
fall	fell
fight	fought
meet	met
pay	paid
send	sent

win	won
nouns	*plural*
beach	beaches
child	children
church	churches
foot	feet
mouse	mice
tooth	teeth
university	universities
adjectives	*comparative*
bad	worse
friendly	friendlier
lucky	luckier
sad	sadder
shy	shyer
thin	thinner
ugly	uglier
wet	wetter

2 a) When did you meet your best friend?
 b) Who is the tallest person in your class?
 c) What is the weather like in your country?
 d) How many e-mails do you get every day?
 e) What does your teacher look like?
 f) What were you wearing yesterday?

3 a) He drinks far *too* much beer.
 b) How *did* your parents choose your name?
 c) It *was* raining when I arrived at work.
 d) There were *a* lot of people at the party.
 e) Tiger Woods is *the* greatest golfer of all time.
 f) Venus Williams isn't as tall *as* Shaquille O'Neal.
 g) What *are* the stores like in your hometown?

4 a) was sleeping b) the most c) don't we go
 d) air e) much f) few g) got
 h) were driving i) saw j) looks k) don't we
 l) got m) continued n) turned o) said
 p) left q) looked r) they got s) enough time
 t) stopped u) Can you ask

5 a) do you weigh?
 b) many people at the party.
 c) lot of sleep last night.
 d) him two years ago.
 e) you wearing yesterday?
 f) more attractive than Michael.
 g) as old as Cathy.
 h) best golfer in the world.

6 a) 5 b) 3 c) 6 d) 4 e) 2 f) 1 g) 8 h) 7

Vocabulary

1 a) F b) F c) T d) T e) T f) F g) T
 h) T i) T j) F k) F l) F

2 a) out b) up c) up d) out e) down f) up
 g) up h) up

3 a) noisy b) improve c) track d) funeral
 e) invent f) village g) earn
 Hidden words: UNIT FIVE

4 a) have b) have c) having d) get e) make

f) got g) get h) make i) make

5 a) danger b) decision c) description
 d) fashion e) introduction f) luck
 g) marriage h) noise i) operation j) religion
 k) romance l) success

6 a) description b) choice c) operation
 d) success e) danger f) marriage g) fashion
 h) introduction

7 I went out on *an unusual* date with my boyfriend yesterday. He took me to a very *cheap* restaurant and I had the *worst* meal of my life. The food was *terrible*, and the wine was the *least* expensive on the menu. John is *a difficult* man to be with: he's *poor* and *unattractive*, and he can be very *boring*. When he asked me to marry him, I said…

8 husband's appearance average height extremely mustache intelligent friend complete opposite overweight cheeseburger

---

6 *Shop*

Grammar

1 a) to b) to c) for d) for e) to f) to g) to

2 a) I told him your secret—I hope that's O.K.
 b) I lent her my car.
 c) Philip made her a delicious dinner.
 d) Why don't you get her some candy?
 e) You need to show him/her your bus pass.
 f) Give him/her the ticket.
 g) I sent him/her a letter last week.

3 a) correct b) correct
 c) I gave ~~for~~ my nephew a gold pen for his birthday.
 d) We've brought ~~to~~ you some really good news.
 e) correct f) correct
 g) The salesclerk explained ~~me~~ the advantages of speed dialing.
 h) She described ~~us~~ the new leopard-skin miniskirt she had bought.

4 a) He often drives me crazy.
 b) I hardly ever wear perfume.
 c) She usually doesn't arrive on time.
 d) I have never been to a garden center.
 e) She is rarely positive about her husband.
 f) We don't often celebrate Valentine's Day.
 g) I'm normally not very good at choosing presents.

5 a) to stay b) spending c) surfing d) eating
 e) to look f) to have g) going

Reading

1 The following sentence does not belong: "It's often a good idea to try on one or two pairs."

2 1 d) 2 b) 3 c) 4 c) 5 c) 6 a)

Vocabulary

1 a) evening gown   b) engagement ring
c) shopping bag   d) clothing store
e) cell phones   f) price tag
g) electronic gadget

2

material	pattern
cotton	check
denim	patterned
leather	plain
silk	striped
synthetic	
wool	

3 a) skirt   b) bracelet   c) earrings   d) necklace
e) tie   f) top   g) pants

4 a) 2   b) 7   c) 3   d) 4   e) 8   f) 1   g) 5   h) 6

Pronunciation

a) Nine hundred twenty-five
b) Two thousand nine hundred forty
c) Thirteen thousand eight hundred twenty-two
d) A hundred eighteen thousand seven hundred fifty
e) Two million seven hundred fifty thousand six hundred five
f) Fifty million four hundred twenty-nine
g) Nine hundred ninety-nine million nine hundred ninety-nine thousand nine hundred ninety-nine

---

7 Job

Grammar

1

simple verb form	simple past	past participle
break	broke	broken
cut	cut	cut
drop	dropped	dropped
hold	held	held
know	knew	known
leave	left	left
pay	paid	paid
run	ran	run
see	saw	seen
stand	stood	stood
tell	told	told
travel	traveled*	traveled*
try	tried	tried

traveled (US English), *travelled* (UK English)

2 a) has had   b) Have you ever worked
c) have never been   d) has ever happened
e) have hated   f) Have you ever thought
g) have always wanted

3 a) this week   b) yesterday   c) last summer
d) this week   e) over the years   f) recently
g) today

4 a) ever had / have ever had
b) have always been
c) have never eaten   d) started   e) needed
f) had   g) thought   h) have always liked
i) have never made   j) smelled
k) were   l) often had   m) was   n) shouted
o) have you sold   p) have not sold
q) arrested   r) was

Listening

1 c) a chef   e) a conductor

2 a) Yes   b) Yes   c) No   d) No   e) No   f) Yes
g) No   h) Yes   i) Yes   j) No   k) No

3 a dishwasher

Vocabulary

1 accountant   actor   artist   banker   chef   doctor
farmer   hairdresser   midwife   nanny   nurse
photographer   pilot   secretary   teacher   vet
waitress

2 a) career   b) employee   c) staff   d) resignation
e) salary   f) living   g) company   h) application

3 a) 4   b) 5   c) 2   d) 6   e) 3   f) 1

4 a) broken   b) given   c) worked   d) had
e) earned   f) eaten   g) happened

Writing

1 1 i)   2 n)   3 a)   4 m)   5 b)   6 c)   7 d)
8 g)   9 e)   10 k)   11 j)   12 f)   13 h)   14 l)

---

8 Rich

Grammar

1 a) I'm tired. I'm going to have an early night.
b) What about tomorrow? Are you *going* to be free in the evening?
c) Yes, but I'm *not* going to go out. I want to watch TV.
d) Are you going *to* come with me to my parents' house on Saturday?
e) No, I'm going to *see* Tony and Carla this weekend.
f) Veronica, when are we going *to* get married?
g) I've already told you, Barry. We're never *going to* get married.

2 a) F   b) F   c) P   d) P   e) F   f) P   g) F

3 a) He's having lunch with his mom at 1 o'clock.
b) He's giving an interview at the MTV studios at 3 o'clock.
c) He's flying to Los Angeles at 6 o'clock.
d) He's attending the American Music Awards ceremony at 8 o'clock.

4   a) What are you going to have for lunch tomorrow?
    b) What are you going to do after school?
    c) What are you going to do this weekend?
    Students' own answers

Reading

1   Getty Helps Troubled Conservative Party

2   a) F   b) T   c) T   d) F   e) F   f) F   g) F
    h) F   i) T   j) F

3   a) election   b) donated   c) grateful   d) addicts
    e) kidnapped   f) mind   g) fortune   h) handed

Vocabulary

1   a) inherited   b) bill   c) rent   d) profit
    e) save   f) exchange rate   g) pension
    h) invest   i) make

2   a) band   b) single   c) fans   d) canceled
    e) charts   f) concert   g) album   h) gigs
    i) tour   j) lead

3   a) 3   b) 7   c) 8   d) 5   e) 4   f) 6   g) 1   h) 2

4   a) decision   b) disaster   c) employment
    d) freedom   e) performance   f) popularity
    g) retirement   h) equipment

Writing

1   a) 4   b) 7   c) 3   d) 6   e) 1   f) 8   g) 2   h) 5

Pronunciation

1   a) Who's Gonna Stop the Rain? (Anastacia)
    b) Your Time is Gonna Come (Led Zeppelin)
    c) I'm Gonna Be Alright (Jennifer Lopez)
    d) It's Gonna Be Me ('N Sync)

2   *Wanna* is short for "want to."

9 Rules

Grammar

1   1 a)   2 b)   3 b)   4 b)   5 a)   6 a)

2   a) People could choose between the army and the navy.
    b) All new soldiers had to have a medical examination.
    c) You couldn't join the army if you had a physical handicap.
    d) You couldn't have long hair in the army.
    e) Women didn't/did not have to do military service.
    f) Foreigners didn't/did not have to register for military service.

3   a) We had to wait in line for two hours./We had to wait for two hours in line./We had to spend two hours waiting in line.

    b) You should arrive at the museum early in the morning.
    c) We didn't have to get a guide.
    d) You shouldn't go there with young children.
    e) On Wednesdays, you don't have to pay for the museum./to visit the museum.
    f) We couldn't/weren't allowed to take any photos.

Listening

1   a) F   b) F   c) T   d) T   e) F

2   The following should have checks:
    b)   c)   d)   e)   g)   h)

Vocabulary

1   a) sensible   b) lazy   c) sensitive   d) optimistic
    e) cheerful   f) insecure   g) silly

2   a) Elementary   b) class   c) Subjects   d) take
    e) fourteen to seventeen   f) final   g) students

3   a) about   b) for   c) with   d) on   e) to   f) of
    g) for   h) in

4   a) 7 physics
    b) 3 economics
    c) 4 geography
    d) 6 math
    e) 2 chemistry
    f) 1 biology
    g) 5 history

5   a) advice   b) exactly   c) friendly
    d) childhood   e) embarrassing   f) foreigner
    g) traditional

Writing

1   a) 8   b) 10   c) 7   d) 6   e) 4   f) 2   g) 9
    h) 1   i) 3   j) 5

2

contracted form	full form
I'm	I am
I haven't	I have not
I've	I have
I don't	I do not
that's	that is
I'll	I will

Pronunciation

a) could not → couldn't
b) does not → doesn't
c) does not → doesn't
d) does not → doesn't
e) should not → shouldn't
f) cannot → can't
g) did not → didn't
h) did not → didn't
i) do not → don't
j) do not → don't

10 Review 2

Grammar

1 1 d) 2 b) 3 c) 4 a) 5 b) 6 d)

2 a) Did you ~~to~~ have to wear a uniform in high school?
b) Have you been ~~go~~ to the movies recently?
c) I couldn't ~~to~~ invite my friends to my house.
d) I don't bother ~~to~~ going to supermarkets anymore.
e) I'm ~~not~~ definitely not going to forget my real friends.
f) Matt is having ~~eat~~ lunch with Madonna and Guy on Monday.
g) My husband bought ~~to~~ me a silver bracelet for my birthday.
h) She is ~~not~~ hardly ever at home in the evenings.
i) I ~~was~~ wrote an angry letter to the bank yesterday.
j) There shouldn't ~~to~~ be different rules for men and women.
k) We ~~were~~ studied this with our teacher last year.

3 *Suggested answers*
a) Last week, I lent my brother 20 dollars./ Last week, I lent 20 dollars to my brother.
b) Unfortunately, I couldn't finish the exercise./ Unfortunately, I wasn't able to finish the exercise.
c) My mother taught me Spanish.
d) We did not have to/need to take the car.
e) She hardly ever arrives on time.
f) What are you doing/going to do this weekend?
g) A man in the street sold me a cheap watch.
h) I think you should/ought to call him.
i) You don't have to/need to pay for the museum after five o'clock./ You don't have to/need to pay to get into the museum after five o'clock.

4 a) than b) never/not c) told d) could
e) not f) have g) you h) her
i) must/have to/should/can j) to k) like
l) have m) me n) tell o) living/being
p) ever

Vocabulary

1 a) marathon b) runners c) give up
d) fortunately e) lift f) stadium g) winner
h) photograph i) gold medal j) found out
k) realized l) achieved m) dishonest
n) noisy o) allowed

2 a) at b) in c) about d) to e) of f) of
g) on h) for i) about j) of k) of l) for
m) over n) In o) for p) about q) of
r) up s) of t) into

3 a) confident b) famous c) friendly
d) miserable e) mysterious f) stressful
g) successful h) traditional

4 *Across*
1 stage 3 ice 5 castle 9 ring 10 album
11 wet 12 at first 14 upset 15 vote
18 opens up 20 romantic 22 army 23 acted
24 earning 25 far 26 alive 27 thin
28 ladder 29 add 30 waste

Down
1 strawberry 2 gig 4 Chinese 6 Egypt
7 statue 8 marathon 13 sofa 16 appearance
17 disagree 19 name 21 striped 22 advice
24 equal 27 tea

11 Smile

Grammar

1 a) Never call the waiter *garçon* in a French cafe.
b) Always cross your knife and fork after a meal in Italy.
c) Never eat with your left hand in north Africa.
d) Always give a tip to New York taxi drivers.
e) Always try to speak Spanish if you are a tourist in Mexico.
f) Always be on time if you are invited to someone's home in the United States.
g) Always take off your shoes when you go into a Japanese house.
h) Never kiss your colleagues at business meetings in China.

2 a) correct
b) I think I'll stay up ~~the evening~~ and watch the late-night movie on TV.
c) correct
d) correct
e) Why don't you sit down ~~the chair~~ and rest?
f) They decided to split up ~~their relationship~~ after three years together.
g) correct

3 a) Would you like to try it on?
b) you'll soon get over it.
c) I think I threw it away!
d) you really take after her!
e) could you turn it down, please?
f) I'm not going to take it off
g) You have to give them up immediately!

Reading

1 b) paragraph 4 c) paragraph 1
d) paragraph 2 e) paragraph 5

2 a) T b) F c) F d) F e) T f) F g) T
h) T

3 a) (the portrait of) the Mona Lisa
b) the merchant

c) (the portrait of) the Mona Lisa
d) the Louvre
e) the American expert
f) these features (the corners of the eyes and mouth)

Vocabulary

1 a) eyebrow b) eyelash c) cheek
  d) mustache e) lip f) teeth

3 a) confident b) loyal c) miserable
  d) mysterious e) secretive f) strong
  g) warm

4 a) fill out   *an application / a form / ~~a mess~~*
  b) get over   *an illness / a problem / ~~money~~*
  c) give up   *music lessons / smoking / ~~a coat~~*
  d) put on   *~~a form~~ / some music / your shoes*
  e) turn on   *a computer / ~~smoking~~ / the TV*
  f) take off   *your clothes / ~~a test~~ / your watch*
  g) turn up   *~~a job~~ / the music / the volume*

5 a) down b) away c) after d) off e) up
  f) with g) away

Writing

1 The first invitation is from Colonel and Mrs. Peacock. It is for their daughter's wedding. The wedding is on April 1.

The second invitation is from David and Jeff. It is for a New Year's Eve party. The party is on December 31.

The third invitation is from Helen. It is inviting Brenda to Helen's office Christmas party. The party is on December 21.

2 1 b) 2 d) 3 a) 4 f) 5 c) 6 e)

12 Rebel

Grammar

1 a) He *has* a poster of Anna Kournikova on his bedroom wall.
  b) How many countries *have* nuclear weapons?
  c) correct
  d) correct
  e) She *had* a boyfriend who worked in a circus last year.
  f) correct
  g) correct
  h) She *has* pink hair and a ring in her nose.

2 a) remains b) is best known c) plays
  d) died e) was brought up f) went
  g) was accepted h) was seen i) was given
  j) became k) was killed

3 a) landed, was named
  b) was defeated, became
  c) was published, became

d) traveled, was welcomed
e) joined, was defeated
f) won, was caught
g) fought, was killed
h) was announced, did not believe

Listening and reading

1 Peaceful Demonstration Turns Violent

2 a) done b) given c) killed d) set
  e) attacked f) sent

3 a) demonstrators b) a peaceful protest
  c) leaflets d) anti-police e) a fairer system
  f) the law g) a group h) Our cause

Vocabulary

1 a) about b) into c) against d) in e) of
  f) with g) away h) out i) at j) to

2 a) Police officers b) high unemployment
  c) fur coats d) recycling center
  e) public transportation f) plastic bags
  g) nuclear weapons h) protest marches

3 a) organization b) fascination c) separation
  d) legalization e) decision f) exhibition
  g) reduction h) decorations

4

1	2	3	4	5	6	7	8
g	a	c	b	f	h	d	e

Writing

1 a) small number b) Most c) several
  d) large number e) none f) a few
  g) nobody h) majority

Pronunciation

Mi<u>ss</u>ions, ambi<u>ti</u>ons, tradi<u>ti</u>ons, per<u>miss</u>ions, condi<u>ti</u>ons, competi<u>ti</u>ons, Associa<u>ti</u>ons, corpora<u>ti</u>ons, obliga<u>ti</u>ons, Demon<u>stra</u>tions, appli<u>ca</u>tions, popula<u>ti</u>ons, destina<u>ti</u>ons

13 Dance

Grammar

1 a) since b) for c) for d) since e) since
  f) for g) since h) for
  Students' own answers

2 a) bought b) been c) gone d) sung, seen
  e) met f) eaten

3 a) has been a fashion model since
  b) has been famous since
  c) have been married for
  d) has been in New York since
  e) have known him for
  f) has he had

4 a) have been b) have been building
c) have been saving d) have been dancing
e) has been f) has had

Reading

1

Billy Elliot	Jamie Bell
Billy's father	Gary Lewis
Billy's brother	Jamie Draven
Billy's grandmother	Jean Heywood
The dance teacher	Julie Walters
Michael	Stuart Wells

2 a) 7 b) 1 c) 3 d) 2 e) 6 f) 5 g) 4

3 a) ✓ b) ✓ c) ✗ d) ✓ e) ✓ f) ✗
g) ✓ h) ✗ i) ✗ j) ✓

4 a) best-known b) follow in his footsteps
c) ridiculous d) express yourself
e) a key moment f) for all tastes

Vocabulary

1 a) flamenco b) waltz c) samba
d) rock 'n' roll e) reggae f) pop

2 a) nightlife b) clubs c) dance floors
d) room e) live f) DJ g) House h) stage

3 a) at b) on c) on d) at e) at f) on
g) on h) at

4 a) pretty b) guy c) reckon d) beat
e) broke f) laid-back

5 a) about b) toward c) for d) for e) on
f) of g) with

Writing

1 1 c) 2 a) 3 b)

2 a) because of b) because c) because
d) because of e) because f) because of

---

14 Call

Grammar

1 1 a) 2 c) 3 c) 4 b) 5 a)

2 a) Do you think he will return my call?
b) Can you remember what time the meeting is?
c) Could you tell me how much a beer costs?
d) Do you know if he gave her the message?
e) Do you know what "worried sick" means?
f) Could you tell me what you think of my outfit?
g) Can you remember who you spoke to?

3 a) Can you remember where I put my car keys?
b) Do you know how much this costs in dollars?
c) Could you tell me where the theater is?
d) Do you think it is against the law?
e) Do you know if she is married?

Listening

1 a) Conversation 2
b) Conversation 1
c) Conversation 3

2 a) Is…there, please? 1
b) Who's calling? 1
c) I'd like to speak to… 2
d) Could I speak to…? 3
e) Sorry, she's not in right now. 1
f) Thank you for calling. 2
g) I'll connect you. 3
h) Can you tell her I called, please? 1
i) Please hold. 2
j) You have the wrong extension. 3
k) Can I take a message? 1
l) No one is available to take your call. 3

Vocabulary

1 a) operator b) dialed c) extension
d) message e) voice mail f) call g) cell phone
h) connection

2 a) told b) said c) said d) asked e) told
f) said g) asked h) told i) said

3 a) on b) at c) on d) at e) in f) on g) in
h) in i) at j) on

4 a) hang b) pick c) connect d) give
e) come f) get g) run h) call

5

1	2	3	4	5	6	7	8
b	g	c	a	f	h	e	d

Writing

1 1 Mr. *Lopez* from *Credit* Bank called—call him back: (555) 450-*1010*.

2 *Richard* called—he's canceled tennis tonight. Next *week* O.K.

3 *Mary* from AWOL Travel says your *tickets* for Mexico City are ready.

2 *Suggested answers*
Amy called about your advertisement for a babysitter. Call back after 6 o'clock—899-5590.

Brenda called—meeting at the office with someone from the legal department 8 o'clock tomorrow morning. Very important.

15 Review 3

Grammar

1

verbs	past participle
agree	agreed
carry	carried
commit	committed
enjoy	enjoyed
hide	hidden
hold	held
kidnap	kidnapped
rob	robbed
run	run
throw	thrown

nouns	plural
factory	factories
illness	illnesses
knife	knives
luxury	luxuries
roof	roofs
toe	toes
wife	wives

adjectives	superlative
bossy	bossiest
deep	deepest
easy	easiest
good	best
messy	messiest
rude	rudest
silly	silliest
wide	widest

2
a) Do you like James Bond movies?
b) Are you thinking of going out tonight?
c) Have you gone abroad this year?
d) How long have you been living here?
e) Have you been to the movies recently?
f) Would you like me to help you?

3
a) A Che poster *was* pinned on his wall when he was a student.
b) How long *have* you been studying English?
c) I *have* been a DJ for two years.
d) I *was* wondering *if* you could lend me your car.
e) Is *it* O.K. if I bring my friend?
f) Rosie *is/was* looking for a new place to live.
g) She *was* kidnapped by a revolutionary group.

4
a) have you been   b) for   c) told   d) to help
e) looked   f) buying   g) allowed   h) thought
i) to go   j) tell   k) thought of him   l) put it on
m) was asked   n) have come   o) he is
p) replied   q) Get in   r) at   s) have been waiting
t) for

5
a) Don't be late."
b) pardoned by President Clinton in 2001.
c) took the photo of Che.
d) been to the movies in a month.
e) been a DJ for two years.
f) like me to call you later?
g) you could take a message.

6   a) 8   b) 1   c) 7   d) 3   e) 6   f) 4   g) 2   h) 5

Vocabulary

1   a) T   b) F   c) T   d) T   e) F   f) F   g) T
h) T   i) T   j) T   k) T   l) F   m) F

2   a) over   b) up   c) up   d) through   e) up
f) off   g) out   h) out

3   a) enjoyed   b) confident   c) inherit   d) starred
e) illness   f) organic   g) naughty
Hidden word: DECISION

4   a) got   b) got   c) had   d) had   e) make
f) had   g) get   h) made   i) make

5   a) cruelty   b) demonstration   c) difficulty
d) education   e) explanation   f) explosion
g) information   h) legalization   i) mystery
j) pollution   k) science   l) tradition

6   a) confidence   b) education   c) information
d) demonstration   e) legalization   f) difficulty
g) explanation   h) cruelty

7   It was a *cold, wet* day, and we were driving *fast* down a *narrow* street in the town. My husband is a *careless* driver, and he *never* stops at red lights. Suddenly, another car drove into the *front* of our Mercedes. *Unfortunately*, my husband is a very *violent* man, and he's always very *rude*. He got out of the car…

8   usual   worried   nervously   finally   carefully   absolutely   wrong   replied   scream   people   concert

16 Lifestyle

Grammar

1
a) you *will* be relaxed and positive about life.
b) you *will* feel younger and healthier.
c) your energy levels *will* be much higher.
d) relationships with your friends *will* be happier.
e) your general fitness *will* improve.
f) you *will* change the way you think about food.
g) your friends *will* think you look wonderful.

2   *Suggested answers*
a) He won't be relaxed and positive about life.
b) He probably won't feel younger and healthier.
c) His energy levels definitely won't be much higher.
d) Relationships with his friends definitely won't be happier.
e) His general fitness probably won't improve.
f) He won't change the way he thinks about food.
g) His friends definitely won't think he looks wonderful.

3 a) comes b) will say c) is d) will think
  e) loses f) eats g) asks

4 a) isn't, will take
  b) will have, doesn't speak
  c) get, will call
  d) are, 'll look
  e) 'll go, want
  f) isn't, 'll find
  g) 'll tell, get

Reading

1 Genetically Modified Fast Food *paragraph C*
  The Danger to the Environment *paragraph B*
  What is Added to Your Fast Food? *paragraph A*

2 a) 2 b) 6 c) 1 d) 3 e) 4 f) 5

3 a) ingredients b) health c) Research
  d) packaging e) environment f) modified

Vocabulary

1 a) a healthy life b) your fitness c) fit
  d) a walk e) weight f) yoga g) stress
  h) vacation

2 a) spinach b) grape c) trout d) shrimp
  e) pepper f) garlic g) carrot h) eggplant
  i) cucumber j) lettuce k) chicken l) sausage

3 b) 3 c) 6 d) 8 e) 2 f) 7 g) 1 h) 4

4 a) calorie b) junk c) recipe d) snack
  e) starving f) vitamins

5 a) not my cup of tea b) packed in like sardines
  c) a piece of cake d) spill the beans

Pronunciation

a) break b) peach c) friend d) receive
e) abroad f) youth g) mountain

---

17 Animals

Grammar

1 a) who b) who c) that d) that e) who
  f) who g) that h) who

2 a) that b) that c) – d) that e) – f) that
  g) that h) –

3 a) would you try b) came c) invited
  d) would you do e) asked f) would you feel
  g) would you give
  Students' own answers

Listening

1 The order is: d), b), c), a).

2 1 b) 2 a) 3 a) 4 b)

Vocabulary

1 ant bear camel cat cheetah cow deer
  dog dolphin elephant fish giraffe hamster
  horse iguana kangaroo mosquito parrot
  pig rat reptile snake spider turtle

2 a) dog b) spider c) snake d) kangaroo
  e) parrot f) giraffe g) cheetah h) horse
  (*Camel* is also correct.)

3 a) wait b) deer c) write d) bear e) weight

4 a) bored b) afraid c) big d) worried
  e) tired f) approve g) fascinated h) think

---

18 Weird

Grammar

1 1 a) 2 b) 3 b) 4 a) 5 a) 6 a)

2 a) had seen b) had missed c) had had
  d) hadn't studied e) had been engaged

3 a) had arrived b) spoke c) discovered
  d) had been e) was f) was g) discovered
  h) had gotten married i) had died j) heard

4 a) heard b) realized c) had died
  d) looked e) asked f) had lost g) took
  h) had left i) had died j) discovered

Reading

1 1 d) 2 e) 3 a) 4 f) 5 c) 6 b)

2

1	2	3	4	5	6	7	8
e	c	a	f	g	h	b	d

Vocabulary

1 a) many b) old c) well d) often e) long
  f) far g) much
  Students' own answers

2 a) take b) take c) make d) have
  e) have f) take g) make h) make

3 a) jealous b) embarrassed c) in a bad mood
  d) proud e) sad f) on top of the world
  g) excited h) frightened

4 a) flight b) investigation c) explanations
  d) permission e) description f) development
  g) confidence

Pronunciation

a) Yes, I've seen about a *thousand*.
b) The first crop circle was seen in *1980*.
c) Actually, we found it in the *morning*.
d) No, we think it was made by *aliens*.
e) Yes, it's about a *half a mile wide*!
f) No, I've *never* seen one like *this*.

19 Wheels

Grammar

1
a) The roads used to be quiet and safe.
b) no change
c) I used to be very proud of my bike.
d) I used to clean it every day.
e) My best friend used to be a boy named Tom.
f) no change g) no change h) no change

2
a) If I were you, I'd choose a good language school. / I'd choose a good language school if I were you.
b) You could look for a job there.
c) Why don't you stay with an American family?
d) If I were you, I'd go in the winter./I'd go in the winter if I were you.

3 *Suggested answers*
a) The roads used to be less busy.
b) There used to be fewer people.
c) There didn't use to be advertisements.
d) There didn't use to be as many tourists.
e) There didn't use to be taxis.

Listening

1 Speaker 1 b)
Speaker 2 c)
Speaker 3 a)

2

	Speaker 1	Speaker 2	Speaker 3
What color is it?	✗	white	red
What special features does it have?	✓ beds kitchen table john television	✓ black windows shiny wheels cocktail bar DVD	✓ car stereo
How fast does it go?	✗	✗	✓ 250 mph
Where would you like to go in your car?	✓ Michigan	✓ Hollywood	✓ Monte Carlo
Who would you take with you?	✓ grand-children	✓ friends	✓ Jennifer Lopez

Vocabulary

1
a) steering, gears b) belts, seats
c) engine, hood d) tire, trunk
e) windshield, wipers

2
a) Public transportation b) air conditioning
c) hairstyle d) traffic jam e) fast food
f) health care g) summer vacation
h) driver's license

3
a) dangerously b) partly c) heavily
d) casually e) closely f) intelligently
g) specially h) abroad

4
a) powerful b) spacious c) electric
d) polluted e) aggressive f) considerate
g) angry h) safe i) wise

Writing

1 to give advice about traveling in Florida

2

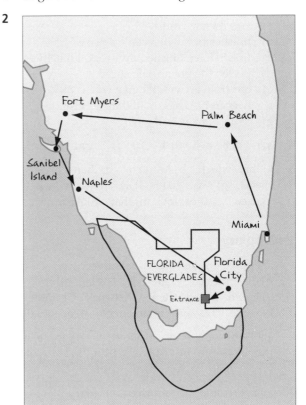

3 I suggest that you... You could...
why don't you...

Pronunciation

1 The second speaker sounds more positive. She uses a higher tone of voice.

20 Review 4

Grammar

1 1 d) 2 c) 3 b) 4 b) 5 a) 6 d)

2 a) We will take a break when we ~~will~~ finish this exercise.
   b) That's the man I told you about ~~him~~.
   c) I have a friend who ~~she~~ got married last week.
   d) They ~~were~~ used to live in Monterrey.
   e) If you read more books, your English ~~it~~ would improve.
   f) I would ~~to~~ see a doctor if I were you.
   g) I hope I will ~~to~~ find a good job soon.
   h) When he had finished breakfast, he ~~had~~ left for work.
   i) She used to have ~~wearing~~ long blond hair.
   j) Why don't you speak to someone who ~~he~~ understands the problem?

3 a) you review Unit 17?"
   b) finishes first will receive a prize.
   c) finish/have finished my work, I'll help you.
   d) peeled the potato, she sliced it.
   e) our train arrives, I'll give you a call.
   f) lives in L.A. has invited me to visit.
   g) to be a green field.

4 a) 6 b) 8 c) 5 d) 4 e) 9 f) 7 g) 1 h) 2 i) 3

5 a) that/which b) to c) in d) than e) he
   f) was g) was h) of i) as j) that/which
   k) used l) after/for m) that n) At o) was

Vocabulary

1 a) opposite b) character c) career
   d) disapproved e) lifestyle f) relationship
   g) lasted h) separated i) network j) trouble
   k) while l) escape m) incidents n) eventually

2 a) of b) with/in/of c) about/of d) up e) in
   f) as g) in h) In i) about j) To k) to l) of
   m) of n) to o) for p) of q) on

3 a) aggressive b) amused c) angry
   d) believable e) jealous f) spacious
   g) surprising

4 Maggie was always *unlucky* with men, and one day she contacted a dating service. She was looking for a *weak* personality because she was very *shy* herself. A week later, the dating service found a man. They said he had *little* in common with her and they were sure their first date would be a *failure*.

Before going out, Maggie *forgot* to brush her teeth and put on her new perfume. She smelled *awful*! Feeling really *nervous*, she arrived at the restaurant, which was almost *full*. Then, she saw him, sitting at a table with a *silly* expression on his face. It was definitely him. It was her *previous* husband!

5 *Across*
1 windshield wiper 6 low 8 treats 9 eat
10 ate 11 abroad 14 create 15 studio
16 notice 18 carrot 19 won't do 21 fur
22 pig 23 shrimp 24 add 25 air conditioning

Down
2 I don't think so 3 snake 4 lettuce 5 dead
7 message 12 road 13 all of a sudden
15 strange 17 I had 18 chopped 19 will
20 igloo